Steven Caney's
**TOY BOOK**

Steven Caney's

# TOY BOOK

WORKMAN PUBLISHING COMPANY
NEW YORK CITY

WP

ISBN: 0-911104-15-1
       0-911104-17-8 (pbk.)

Cover design: Tedd Arnold
Cover illustration: Tim Lewis
Book design: Bernard Springsteel
Book photographs: Steven Caney
Book illustration: Arielle Mather

Workman Publishing Company, Inc.
1 West 39th Street
New York, NY 10018

Manufactured in the United States of America

First printing, November 1972
20  19  18  17  16  15

*To Jennifer, Noah, and the refrigerator carton*

My appreciation to Rick Culkins and Peter Bull for their enthusiasm and inventiveness, to my wife Shelly for her generous assistance and tolerance of the dining room table's being used as a workbench, and to all the kids who helped: Dana Bates, Amy Bentley, Jennifer and Noah Caney, Caity Conley, Gary, Patty, Barbie, and Mary Culkins, Mandy and Carol Degnon, David, Daniel, and Jodie Hurwitz, Karen Kunstenaar, Mark Lemmerman, Arthur, Peter, and Sally Milliken, Michael and Peter Orszag, Ethan Owens, Allison Webb, Jimmy Wooster, and Ingo Szegvari.

*Steven Caney's*
**TOY BOOK**

# TABLE OF CONTENTS

## DISCOVERY TOYS

DONUT BIRD FEEDER . . . . . . . . . . . . . . 22
KAZOO . . . . . . . . . . . . . . . . . . . . . . . . . 25
ANT JAR . . . . . . . . . . . . . . . . . . . . . . . . 27
WATER LENS . . . . . . . . . . . . . . . . . . . . 30
TALEIDOSCOPE . . . . . . . . . . . . . . . . . . 33
DRUM BOX . . . . . . . . . . . . . . . . . . . . . . 36
SUN GOGGLES . . . . . . . . . . . . . . . . . . . 39
ILLUSION CIRCLES . . . . . . . . . . . . . . . 42
MOVIE WHEEL . . . . . . . . . . . . . . . . . . . 45
BAROMETER . . . . . . . . . . . . . . . . . . . . . 49
STRAW HORN . . . . . . . . . . . . . . . . . . . . 52
SUNDIAL . . . . . . . . . . . . . . . . . . . . . . . . 54
WATER SCOPE AND MAGNIFIER . . . . . 57
INSIDE GROWERS . . . . . . . . . . . . . . . . 60
CURDS AND WHEY . . . . . . . . . . . . . . . . 64
CREATURE CAGE . . . . . . . . . . . . . . . . . 66

## PRETENDING TOYS

TUBE TELEPHONE . . . . . . . . . . . . . . . . 70
PRETEND PLAY CUTOUTS . . . . . . . . . . 73
SOAP FLOATS . . . . . . . . . . . . . . . . . . . . 76
SAND COMBS . . . . . . . . . . . . . . . . . . . . 79
MOUSTACHES . . . . . . . . . . . . . . . . . . . . 81

## GAMES

SUBSTITUTION GAME . . . . . . . . . . . . . 86
HEXAFLEXAGON . . . . . . . . . . . . . . . . . 89
GREAT TURTLE RACE . . . . . . . . . . . . . 92
CLOTHESPIN WRESTLERS . . . . . . . . . . 95
RACING SPOOL . . . . . . . . . . . . . . . . . . . 97

RING AND PIN GAME . . . . . . . . . . . . . . 100
NUMBER SQUARE PUZZLE . . . . . . . . . 103

## BUILDING TOYS

BUILDING CIRCLES . . . . . . . . . . . . . . . 108
PEA AND TOOTHPICK BUILDING . . . . . 111
ROPE MACHINE . . . . . . . . . . . . . . . . . . 114
PICTURE PUZZLES . . . . . . . . . . . . . . . . 118
CLIP HANGERS . . . . . . . . . . . . . . . . . . . 121

## ACTION TOYS

CITY KITE . . . . . . . . . . . . . . . . . . . . . . . 124
POCKET PARACHUTE . . . . . . . . . . . . . . 127
TIRE RING SWING . . . . . . . . . . . . . . . . 130
BULL ROARER . . . . . . . . . . . . . . . . . . . . 133
SOAP BUBBLERS . . . . . . . . . . . . . . . . . . 135
PAPER WING AND Z HELICOPTER . . . . 138
DANCING MAN . . . . . . . . . . . . . . . . . . . 141
PROPELLER STICK . . . . . . . . . . . . . . . . 144
MILK CARTON SAILBOAT . . . . . . . . . . 147

## DESIGN TOYS

COLOR JARS . . . . . . . . . . . . . . . . . . . . . 152
CARDBOARD WEAVING . . . . . . . . . . . . 155
ROLLER AND STAMP PRINTING . . . . . . 156
SOAP CRAYONS . . . . . . . . . . . . . . . . . . . 161
CANDY COLOR CIRCLES . . . . . . . . . . . 163
DESIGN BOARD . . . . . . . . . . . . . . . . . . . 166
PAPERBACK SCULPTURE . . . . . . . . . . . 168
PAPER ROLL POTTERY . . . . . . . . . . . . . 171
REFLECTION CARD . . . . . . . . . . . . . . . . 174

# FOREWORD TO PARENTS

Most children have too many toys, and not many of these are very good. Rather than let a child invent, discover or solve mysteries, most store-bought toys confine their play experience to a single purpose, or are too anxious to educate. A child is better off with toys for varying experiences that really work and are fun.

TOY BOOK shows you how to make fifty-one good toys—toys with the ability to be many different things to a child. It is this quality that makes a toy fun for more than a day. A store-bought, child-sized log cabin, for example, is only that to a child—a prefinished log cabin. But a salvaged refrigerator carton can be a house, post office, fire station, rocket ship, train, grocery store—anything a child's imagination will let it be. TOY BOOK toys follow the refrigerator carton in its open-ended spirit and simplicity of design. The toys are fun because they allow the child full imaginative participation—in making them and in playing with them.

•          •          •

The idea of making your own toys is not new. What is new is the idea of buying mass-produced toys. Until the nineteenth century, all toys were handmade—by a parent trying to amuse a child, or by the child himself. With the age of machines and factories, the manufactured toy came into being. There is nothing wrong with a good manufactured toy, of course, but the majority are created with less attention to play value than commercial success. Maybe television advertising of toys is too indiscriminate and too intimidating as it offers the child something new and better, something he can't do without. You know the pattern: too much is available and too much is made of wanting and having, with the result that children think of toys they get as mere possessions. A parent is easy prey to the cuteness, elaborate detail, or even the beautiful packaging of a toy. The manufacturer knew you'd be impressed. But all too often the adornments conceal a toy which isn't fun. The child is not nearly so impressed.

Too many toys are bought by parents caught up in what I call the Guilty Parent Syndrome. Father has been away from home longer than usual, and thinks a new toy should patch things up with the kids. "What did you bring me,

Daddy?" With hugs, kisses, and big smiles, the parent retires with the newspaper while the child goes off to play with another new possession. Unfortunately, the gift-toy peace is usually short-lived because neither parent nor child is really satisfied. What the child wants is the parent to play with, and what the parent wants is to be appreciated for himself. Toys that you make yourself can get the whole family involved.

As for toy or craft kits, the likely alternative, they are no better. They are merely disassembled toys that must be put together again—following instructions. That's fine for the literal-minded parent, but not so good for the child. There is only one way to do it *right,* and where there is only one right way, the child is robbed of creativity and inventiveness. If the child fails, along comes discouragement, and maybe the reluctance to try his hand again.

We need to get away from the idea that toys must come from stores, and that play with those toys must stop inevitably because of boredom. From the beginning, good homemade toys involve kids in a continuous process of doing.

•　　　•　　　•

The toys in TOY BOOK are made from every-day objects—stuff that costs little or nothing. Things like straws, toothpicks, paper plates, string, sticks, clothespins, paper tubes, cups, shirt cardboard, old magazines. Parents should eye household odds and ends with their toy-building potential in mind. Even the strangest things—jar lids, drawer knobs, the plastic holder on a six-pack of soda—can be used imaginatively. A fin-ished toy should cost little or nothing—a child doesn't really care how much his toys cost.

The toy designs are simple and nearly fool-proof—so simple that in the end the toy always works. Still, you never have to worry about doing them precisely. There is a generous "slop factor," so sizes and skills don't have to be exact. If you can't find the suggested material, or it is not cut just right, the toy will most always work anyway, and your child will be happy. A homemade toy can be easily repaired. You built it, so you know how to fix it. Children who fix things feel important. Unlike the store-bought toy, the homemade toy needn't be thrown out if it breaks, or returned for another "potluck" item.

Some of the play projects are based on folk toys and activities many hundreds of years old (there is no such thing as an absolutely new toy). Others are still-popular toys redesigned to be homemade. Whatever their source, the toy recipes were created mostly by me and a band of young co-authors, kids who helped design, build, and photograph. Every toy has been made and played with many times by children of all ages and interests. Altogether we designed nearly two hundred different toys—games, musical instruments, "imaginings," science and nature toys, beach toys, backyard toys and so forth. Each time we thought we'd created the perfect toy, we'd ask ourselves, "Is it really a toy, and not just a craft or experiment? Can it be made successfully by all levels of ability? Is it as fun and safe to play with as make?" Sometimes asking these questions meant going back to the drawing board until the project passed every qualification. *Then* we would decide to include the toy recipe in TOY BOOK

•        •        •

Though the toys in TOY BOOK were designed for a wide age range—starting at about three years—it is generally advisable to match a given toy with its appropriate age group. The age suggestions given should not be considered absolute, however, as they are based on theoretical play interests and abilities of children at different age levels. You know your own child best. If a toy is complicated to build or use, a younger child can become discouraged and reject it. More difficult to predict is the upper age limit for a toy.

Most of the toys can be built by the kids themselves (the directions are addressed to them), but children under six will usually require some supervision. Nearly every child will need some help in getting started, and that's where the parent or someone older comes in.

It's not difficult to play with children—try it. If you have a specific skill or interest, pass it on to the child. Kids like to learn things you know—tips on how to hold a hammer, cut a piece of wood, or use a carving knife. Don't build the toy for the child, however. Though he thinks you can probably do it better than he, he really wants to do it himself—and will, unless you criticize results negatively. Don't expect perfection. For many children, the "doing" is fun enough. A child's conception of workmanship and product is crude and unprofessional, but skills will develop with time, practice, and patience. By the way, playing with her father will not turn a girl into a tomboy, just as playing with his mother will not turn a boy

into a sissy. Not all children are innately creative, but that shouldn't hold them back from inventing and building. Once the child gains the confidence that he can make it—and that it will work—he'll lose his inhibitions about failing and want to experiment, whether by adding a touch of paint, using substitute material, or coming up with his own design.

•        •        •

To make many of these toys, the kitchen might be considered a temporary work space. Any place will do where the child can work without feeling bad about a possible mess—and where his messiness won't upset you. Kids should also have a specific place to deposit their collection of scrounged materials, as the mere presence of such a store can get a child going at inventing. Tinkering, experimenting, and building should be part of everyday activity—don't always leave toy making as a survival plan for rainy days.

Not all homes are equipped with workshop materials, so most of the toys here are designed to be built with no tools, or with simple tools like scissors, pencil, ruler, penknife, hammer, crayons or markers. It is very important that the tools used are real tools. Not only does the child want to use "grown-up tools," but kiddie scissors and saws don't work. They are frustrating, and too often cause children to want to give up the whole project. Cautions about materials and tools are given in the instructions, but be sure that all inherent dangers in equipment are obvious to children. Kids are naturally curious, and will investigate the tools they use. Make sure the items you have given them don't have hidden dangers. Think about the business of hidden danger—it's important. Climbing high on a jungle gym could be dangerous, but the child doing so is well aware of the possibility of falling, and is careful. What the child *doesn't* know can hurt him.

•          •          •

Open the book to any project—it doesn't matter where you begin. Flip through the pages for the toys you find most exciting. Once the choice is made, the child will be bursting with energy and enthusiasm for getting started. Take advantage of that. Help him to get going but, again, let him do the work. The interest and attention span of a child can be quite short unless he feels himself in charge of his own play. He may make a mistake, but trial and error is what it's all about.

When construction is finished, you shouldn't make the child feel precious about his creation—it is not a piece of art to be put on display. The child will want to play with it, maybe give it to a friend, take it apart and put it together again, repair or even destroy it. A good toy doesn't need to last forever, but it does have to be fun.

You might help the child understand how to use his toy, but don't insist. Kids love to invent their own ways of play, and that's all right as long as their play is safe. Children are basically uninhibited in their play, and if a toy is really fun, you'll know it. It's so great to hear a kid say, "I made it myself . . . it really works . . . it's fun."

# SUGGESTED MINIMUM AGES

These are just suggestions; as a parent, you will know your child's interests and abilities best.

|  | Playing | Making |
|---|---|---|
| Donut Bird Feeder | any age | 5+ |
| Kazoo | 3+ | 4+ |
| Ant Jar | any age | 4+ |
| Water Lens | 3+ | 6+ |
| Taleidoscope | 3+ | 6+ |
| Drum Box | 3+ | 7+ |
| Sun Goggles | 5+ | 7+ |
| Illusion Circles | 6+ | 6+ |
| Movie Wheel | 5+ | 6+ |
| Barometer | 7+ | 7+ |
| Straw Horn | 5+ | 5+ |
| Sundial | 6+ | 6+ |
| Water Scope and Magnifier | 4+ | 6+ |
| Inside Growers | any age | 4+ |
| Curds and Whey | any age | 5+ |
| Creature Cage | 3+ | 5+ |
| Tube Telephone | 3+ | 5+ |
| Pretend Play Cutouts | 2+ | 5+ |
| Soap Floats | 1+ | 6+ |
| Sand Combs | 2+ | 6+ |
| Moustaches | 3+ | 4+ |

|  | Playing | Making |
|---|---|---|
| Substitution | 5+ | 6+ |
| Hexaflexagon | 4+ | 7+ |
| Great Turtle Race | 4+ | 5+ |
| Clothespin Wrestlers | 3+ | 5+ |
| Racing Spool | 3+ | 5+ |
| Ring and Pin | 4+ | 6+ |
| Number Square Puzzle | 5+ | 5+ |
| | | |
| Building Circles | 4+ | 6+ |
| Pea and Toothpick Building | 3+ | 3+ |
| Rope Machine | 6+ | 8+ |
| Picture Puzzles | 3+ | 4+ |
| Clip Hangers | 3+ | 4+ |
| | | |
| City Kite | 4+ | 6+ |
| Pocket Parachute | 3+ | 5+ |
| Tire Ring Swing | 2+ | 11+ |
| Bull Roarer | 4+ | 4+ |
| Soap Bubbler | 2+ | 3+ |
| Paper Wing and Z Helicopter | 4+ | 5+ |
| Dancing Man | 6+ | 11+ |
| Propeller Stick | 4+ | 6+ |
| Milk Carton Sailboat | 3+ | 5+ |
| | | |
| Color Jars | 3+ | 3+ |
| Cardboard Weaving | 5+ | 6+ |
| Roller and Stamp Printing | 3+ | 5+ |
| Soap Crayons | 2+ | 6+ |
| Candy Color Circles | any age | 7+ |
| Design Board | 2+ | 4+ |
| Paperback Sculpture | any age | 4+ |
| Paper Roll Pottery | any age | 5+ |
| Reflection Card | 3+ | 4+ |

# DISCOVERY TOYS

# Donut bird feeder

# Donut bird feeder

People like donuts—especially kids—but did you ever think about feeding a donut to the birds? A DONUT BIRD FEEDER can be put out on a windowsill, or hung in a tree, but be sure to keep it away from places that cats and squirrels might reach. Birds make interesting pets, and give you the responsibility of caring for a living thing. Although you really don't "keep" them, the same birds will come back to your feeder—year after year—if they know there will always be food available. If you do start feeding the birds, you have an obligation to keep them supplied with food, especially during the winter months, because some birds will learn to rely on your feeder as their only source of food. You'll soon find that birds do like donuts—plain, chocolate, cinnamon . . .

MATERIALS        TOOLS

2 jar lids        hammer
long nail         pliers
donut
string

## CONSTRUCTION

Find two jar lids about as big around as the donut. Either metal or soft plastic lids will do. Find a "headed" nail about 3 inches long. Make a hole in the center of each lid by hammering the nail through, wiggling it around, and pulling it out. Be sure to work on a scrap piece of wood or on the ground outside—the nail could damage a table or the floor. There are many ways that you can assemble the DONUT BIRD FEEDER, depending on where you want to put it. To hang the

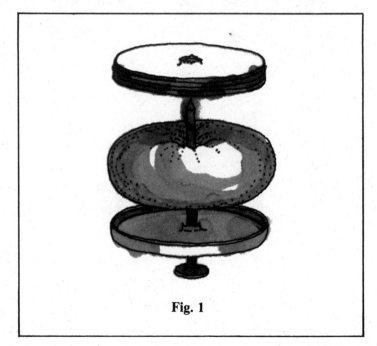

Fig. 1

feeder from a branch or hook, put the nail through one lid, through the donut hole, and then through the other lid, Fig. 1. With pliers, bend the pointed end of the nail sideways to keep it from pulling through the lid. If the nail is too hard to bend, you can hammer the point into a small wood scrap, or wrap a piece of tape around the end. Tie a piece of string below the head of the nail and hang up the feeder, Fig. 2. If you want to use the feeder on a windowsill, assemble the parts in the same way, but instead of bending the nail, tap it lightly into the windowsill. You can also nail the feeder to the underside of a branch. Try to put the feeder in a place that will let you watch the birds. It might take a few days for the birds to find your feeder, but once they do, they will keep coming back. Check often to see if the donut is all eaten and needs to be replaced, and then try another flavor.

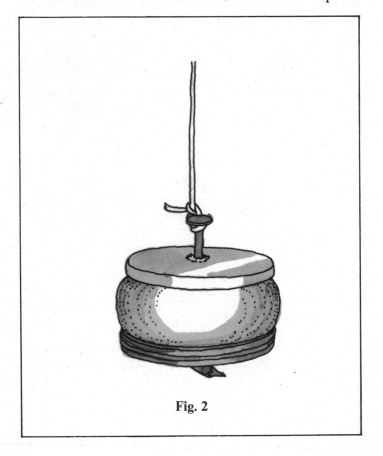

Fig. 2

Kazoo

# Kazoo

Before being sent off to the local music teacher to learn to play some instrument, a kid must first have the incentive to learn, and a comfortable feeling about his musical abilities. The KAZOO is a good instrument to begin experimenting with musical sounds because it can be played instantly, without musical instruction. Singing a tune in "do-do-do-do-do's" is the only talent needed, and that seems to come quite naturally. Even kids who are not musically inclined get excited with the high-pitched raspy sounds they're suddenly able to produce. The KAZOO is a real honest-to-goodness musical instrument—there are even KAZOO bands—and it can be made small enough to fit in your pocket.

## MATERIALS

paper tube
wax paper
rubber band

## TOOLS

pencil

## CONSTRUCTION

Hunt around for a paper tube—any size. Most common are the paper tube centers of paper towels and toilet paper rolls. Tear a piece of wax paper a few inches larger than the tube opening. Aluminum foil will also work fine, but the sound will be higher pitched and not quite as loud. Wrap the wax paper around one open end of the tube. Make sure it's smooth and tight across the opening. Stretch a rubber band around the tube end to hold the wax paper in place. At the same end of the tube, about 1 inch from the end, punch a hole about as round as a pencil. In fact, a pencil is a good thing to punch it with. Now try to play. Hold the open end of the KAZOO around the outside of your mouth. Pucker your lips and begin singing or humming a song in "do's"—"do-do-doodle-oodle, do-do-doodle-oodle, do-do-doodle-oodle-do." Just keep it going with all the songs you know. Try "kazooing" to the music of a record or the radio. Jam with a KAZOO friend.

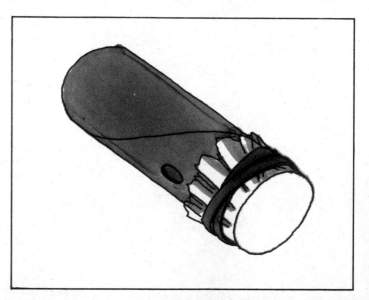

# Ant jar

# Ant jar

Even though parents may cringe at the thought of bringing ants into the house, the little insects lead a rather interesting life, and watching the behavior of an ant colony can be really fascinating. The ants will build an intricate maze of tunnels and rooms in the soil, and busily go about collecting food. It is amazing to see the large pieces of food that a single ant can carry. Did you know that there are queen ants (no king ants), soldier ants, and worker ants—and that the girl ants do all the work? There are things to learn about ants, many of which you can observe in an ANT JAR.

## MATERIALS

2 clear glass jars, one slightly smaller
    than the other
loose or sandy soil
sugar
water

## CONSTRUCTION

The whole idea of making a house for ants is to be able to see what the ants are doing underground. One way to do that is to make the ants' living area a very narrow place which you can see into from the sides. Put the smaller jar, without its lid, upside down into the center of the larger jar, Fig. 1. The space between the two jars should be filled with loose or sandy soil, Fig. 2. Be sure the space is completely filled, but don't pack the soil too tight, or the ants might have a hard time digging. Now you need to find some ants. If your mother can't lead you directly to an available source, try hunting in the back yard, or in the park. To make an ant trap, mix a little bit of sugar with a little water in a small jar or can, and lay the can down on its side on the ground (preferably near an anthill). The ants will go into the jar searching for the sugar food. Cap the jar when you've collected about twenty ants. It is very important that all ants you put in the ANT JAR have come from the same ant colony. Ants from different colonies will not get along together, and will probably fight and kill each other. Put the ants you have collected into the ANT JAR, and screw on the jar lid to keep the ants from escaping. If you don't have a jar lid, a piece of plastic wrap and a rubber band will work fine. Don't worry about the ants getting enough air. When you remove the lid for feeding, plenty of fresh air will enter. Your mother will probably feel much better if you do the transfering of ants outside—just in case a few do get away. Don't crowd too many ants in the ANT JAR—the fewer ants, the more activity there will be. In about a day, the ants will begin to build tunnels and rooms, and you'll be able to see most of what's happening from the outside of the ant house. Once a week *only,* feed the ants a few drops of sugar water, and maybe a few grains of bird or grass seed. Put the food directly on the soil. However tempting it may be, don't overfeed the ants or they might die. Keep the ANT JAR at normal room temperature, and away from radiators, air conditioners, or direct sunlight. If you don't disturb the ANT JAR, the ants will build a complete underground ant city.

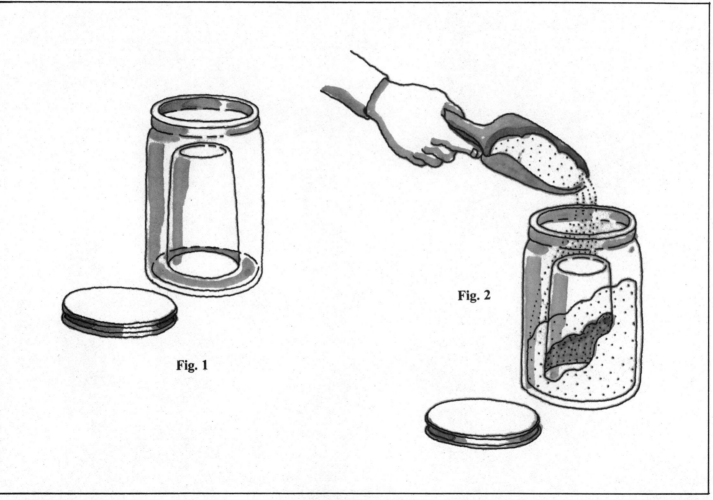

Fig. 1

Fig. 2

# Water lens

# Water lens

Kids like the kind of science that does something. And even though science is something to wonder about, young kids want very little theory, and plenty of results. One of the first tools of science is a magnifier for making regular size things look big, and for examining the incredible detail of small objects. A big lens makes looking easier and more fun, but a big WATER LENS might mean trouble if you spill it in the living room. So the WATER LENS should be used in water play areas like the bathtub, backyard, beach, porch, or in the sink. It really works, and there are lots of things to see and experiments to invent.

## MATERIALS

plastic pail
clear plastic wrap
elastic

## TOOLS

penknife
ball-point pen

## CONSTRUCTION

Find or buy a small soft plastic pail. Paint stores sell inexpensive mixing buckets in 5-pint and 5-quart sizes, and either one will work fine. You can also use a paper bucket, but it will get water soaked and not last very long. With a pen— or other marker—draw three circles around the outside of the pail, and then cut them out, using a penknife or long scissors, Fig. 1. (If you're not good at cutting with a knife, have someone else who is do it for you.) The circle shapes don't have to be exact, but they should be large enough to fit your hand through, and be sure to leave enough of the pail at the top, bottom, and sides so it won't become too flimsy. Cut a piece of clear

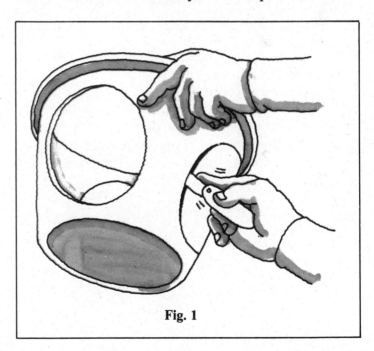

**Fig. 1**

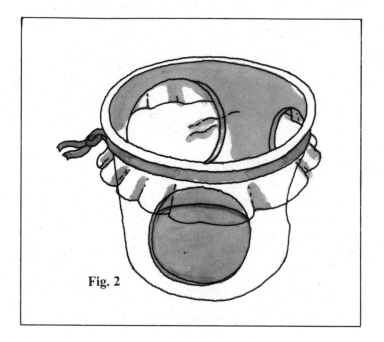

Fig. 2

plastic wrap a few inches larger than the pail opening. Be generous—the size does not have to be exact. Clear food wrap is okay, but a dry cleaner's plastic wrap works best because it stretches a little. Put the plastic wrap loosely over the top of the pail and keep it in place with a snug fitting rubber band made from a knotted piece of elastic, Fig. 2. In a pinch, you can try taping the plastic wrap to the side of the pail. All you need to do now is add water. Slowly pour the water onto the plastic wrap. The water should not be too cold, or condensation will make the lens cloudy. The weight of the water will make the plastic sag, causing it to form the shape of a lens. Add as much water as you can without overflowing. Put objects into the magnifier through the hole cutouts in the side of the pail. You might try experimenting with the amount of magnification by using less water, a larger or smaller pail, and other clear liquids such as cooking oil or corn syrup.

•    •    •

There has been some concern about the safety of the large "stool magnifiers" that are sold in toy stores. The glass lens they use is breakable, and because the lens is always in focus, a stool left in direct sunlight can cause smoldering, and at worst start a fire. The WATER LENS cannot start a fire, and even if it could, as one child noted, "the plastic would melt, dropping the water, which would put out the fire."

# Taleidoscope

Most kids have seen a *kaleidoscope*. You hold a round tube up to an eye, and by rotating one end you see a six-sided pattern of colored plastic bits make beautiful and continuous changes. But what makes the kaleidoscope work is a mystery inside the tube. Not any more. If you were to strip away the outside tube, part of what you'd find inside are two or three mirrorlike surfaces held in a triangular shape. That's what makes things look six-sided. A *TALEIDOSCOPE* is just one set of those three shiny surfaces in a triangle, and you can make anything you want turn into a beautiful, changing pattern. You can look out at a six-sided world, or explore the patterns made by your fingers, a bug, leaf, or the television picture. And if you try putting objects inside the TALEIDOSCOPE, you will have reinvented the kaleidoscope.

## MATERIALS

shiny plastic strips
  (see below)
tape

## TOOLS

(depends)

## CONSTRUCTION

The TALEIDOSCOPE is simply three rectangular pieces of opaque shiny plastic held together

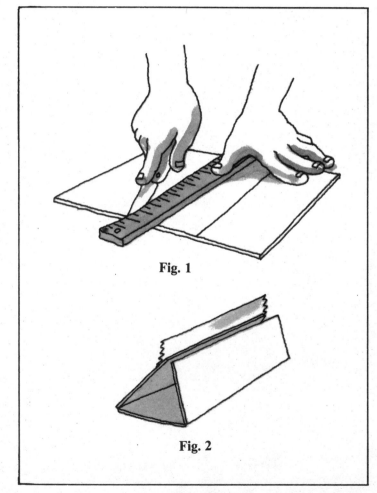

Fig. 1

Fig. 2

34

with tape in the shape of a triangular tube. That's it. Thin acrylic plastic sheet in a dark color works best, although you'd probably have to go to a plastic or glass store to get some. You can also use clear acetate plastic sheet, available at art supply stores. Get the thickest acetate sheet they have. If you use the clear kind, you will have to cover or spray paint one side to make it opaque. If none else is available, you might get by with acetate page covers, the kind used for ring binders. These must also be covered, or preferably spray painted on one side for opaqueness. Cut the plastic into three strips about 2 inches wide and 8 inches long, Fig. 1. Very thin acetate can be cut with a scissors, but to cut heavier plastic you'll need to make a deep scratch line with a knife (using a straight edge for a guide). Bend the plastic, and it will break cleanly along the scratch. Assemble the three plastic strips to form a triangular tube. If you're using painted plastic, make sure the painted surfaces are on the outside. Tape the strips together along the meeting edges, Fig. 2. Any tape will do, but cloth tape makes for a strong and good-looking job. You might experiment with TALEIDOSCOPES of other sizes and proportions. Try making a four-sided TALEIDO-SCOPE and see what happens.

# Drum box

# Drum box

Tap it with your fingers, play it with a spoon. Beat out a rhythm, or play a simple tune. The DRUM BOX is actually a relative of some very old African and Indian hollow log drums. But unlike a log, you can "tune" each side of the DRUM BOX to produce many different tones. Here is a musical instrument that anyone can play. It takes no special skills, and somehow the tone changes always sound just right. After a little "practice," some kids try to invent rhythm patterns and rhythm games, like "what song am I playing?" It's also fun to play along with a record, beat out drum messages, or take to school.

## MATERIALS

4 rectangular pieces of wood, all the same size, about 1/2 to 1 inch thick
nails
glue

## TOOLS

keyhole handsaw (or electric saber saw)
hammer
drill
sandpaper
pencil
ruler

## CONSTRUCTION

Assemble the four pieces of wood to form a box open at two ends, and glue and nail the box together, Fig. 1. Just a little glue always works best. On each surface of the box draw a "slot" pattern something like the ones shown in Fig. 2. The patterns don't have to be exact, and you might want to make up a few experimental patterns of your own. The patterns should not come

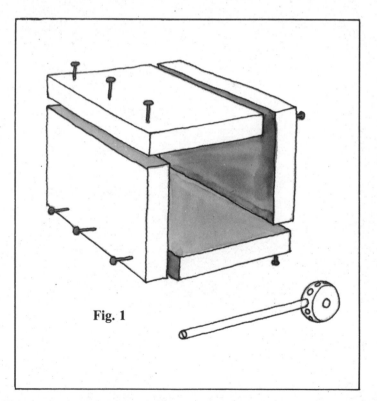

Fig. 1

too close to the edges, or the box might become weak. Follow the pattern with a saw, and cut slots completely through the wood. A good way to start the saw is to drill a starting hole large enough to fit the top of the saw blade. Sandpaper the slots to remove any splinters or rough edges caused by the sawing. Now you can test all the tones of the DRUM BOX by striking each side in different places. There are lots of things you can use for a beater—your knuckles, a big spoon, a short fat stick, or a Tinker Toy baton, Fig. 1. Each DRUM BOX and each beater will make somewhat different tones—some hard, some soft, some terribly sour. If a particular place on the DRUM BOX sounds terrible, or if you just want to change the tone, try cutting the slot a little longer—just 1/4 inch at a time—and test the tone again.

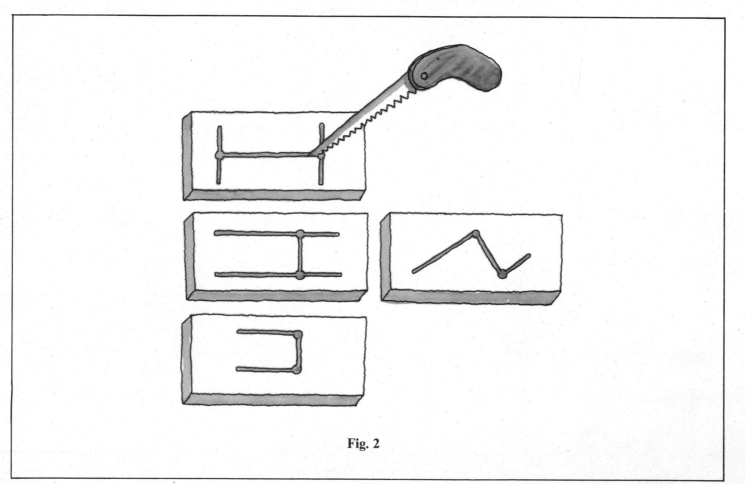

**Fig. 2**

# Sun goggles

# Sun goggles

For hundreds of years the Eskimos have used "sunglasses" that have no lenses—only two narrow slits that keep out most of the bright sunlight. You can make a pair of SUN GOGGLES that work in a similar way, but instead of looking through slits, you look through a lot of small holes. When you wear SUN GOGGLES, you might look more like a man from outer space than an Eskimo, but they really work.

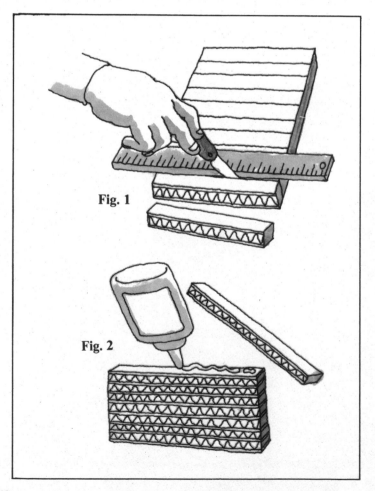

Fig. 1

Fig. 2

| MATERIALS | TOOLS |
|---|---|
| corrugated box | ruler |
| string | pencil |
| paper glue | penknife |

## CONSTRUCTION

Find a corrugated box (the food market has plenty), and cut off a large flat undamaged piece. With a pencil and ruler, mark off about ten or twelve strips 1/2 inch wide and 6 inches long. The corrugations (holes running inside the material) must go across the length of the strips. Cut out the strips with a penknife, using the ruler as a straight-edge guide, Fig. 1. Be sure not to work directly on a table or floor surface, or the knife might make scratches. Work on top of another piece of box material, or on old newspapers. Glue all the strips together, one on top of the other, Fig. 2. Remember that a little bit of glue holds better than a lot, and also makes a neater job. When the glue has dried, cut out a place for your nose. Now tie one end of a piece of string to one side of the goggles by threading it through the corrugations. Loop the free end of the string through the other side of the goggles, but don't tie a knot, Fig. 3. This way the goggles can be adjusted to fit different people. Wear the SUN GOGGLES on a bright sunny day, and you'll discover how they work. You will also discover that you can see only straight ahead, so don't wear them while running or riding your bike.

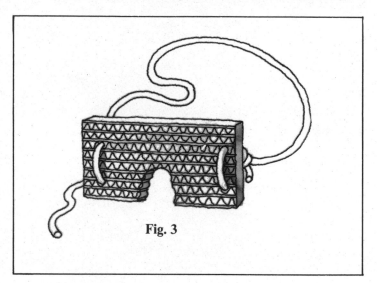

Fig. 3

# Illusion circles

# Illusion circles

Did you ever fool yourself? Sometimes you're fooled by what you see. An old-fashioned barber pole appears to have stripes that move up the pole, but it's only an illusion. Illusions can be surprising, and they sometimes even baffle scientists. The way some of these ILLUSION CIRCLES work still remains a mystery. If you mix red with blue you get purple; green and red make brown. But black and white make brown, yellow, blue, green, purple ... Sound strange? It's an illusion. You can make ILLUSION CIRCLES that will make colors change, and turn black and white into a rainbow of colors. You might be able to convince others that it's magic, but it's all just an illusion.

MATERIALS

cardboard
string
buttons

TOOLS

circle compass
scissors
ruler
crayons
pencil

## CONSTRUCTION

Find a piece of heavy white cardboard. Here are some ideas: the lid from a gift box, a piece of cardboard with white paper glued on the sides, three paper plates glued together. With a circle compass, draw a circle on the cardboard about 4 to 6 inches round. Cut out the circle. Draw any two of the three patterns shown in Fig. 1, one on each side of the disc. The "pielike" pattern is colored in, using two different colors alternately. Crayons or color markers work well. The other two patterns—the strange ones—should be partially colored in black, as in the illustration. Find the exact center of the circle by looking for the point made by the compass. Punch two small holes on opposite sides of the point with a pencil point—about 3/8 inch from the middle works best. It's important that you measure equal space carefully, or the circle might wobble and not work right. Find two big buttons whose holes line up with the holes in the circle. Cut a piece of strong string about 3 feet long. Thread the string through the circle and the buttons, Fig. 2 (a paper clip or pencil point will help with pushing the string through the holes). Tie the two free ends of the string together.

## MAKING IT WORK

Hold one end of the string loop in each hand. The ILLUSION CIRCLE should be in the middle. Have a friend wind up the circle, or do it yourself by holding the string a little slack, and winding the circle against yourself along its edge. When you've wound the circle about ten or fifteen times, pull the string. The circle will spin as the string unwinds, and as it winds again in the opposite direction. By alternately pulling the string taut and giving some slack, you can keep the ILLUSION CIRCLE spinning back and forth.

The illusions will only work well in very bright light—by a window, under a lamp, or outside. Look at the spinning patterns. What happens to the color-striped "pie"? What happens to the black and white pattern? Try staring at the spinning circle for half a minute—did you see color spots? The actual color you see will depend on how fast or slow the disc spins, and how bright the light is. Experiment with the pattern you haven't yet used, Fig. 1, or make up your own patterns of lines, dots, and shapes. Maybe you can guess what the illusion will be.

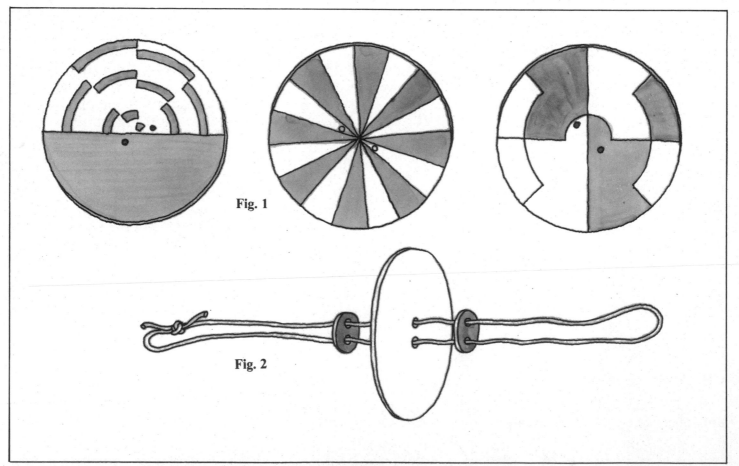

Fig. 1

Fig. 2

Movie wheel

# Movie wheel

Did you ever wonder how a movie camera or a movie projector works? If you take a close look at a piece of movie film, you'll see a series of separate still photographs, each slightly different from the one before it. A movie camera takes each of the still pictures in very quick order—about twenty-four pictures every second; the movie projector shows the pictures back to you at the same speed, so the still pictures look as though they are moving. Movies are really an optical illusion.

The MOVIE WHEEL can be both a movie camera and a movie projector. If you spin the wheel while looking through the slits, any motion you see will appear as a series of still "stop action" pictures. Here are some things to look at that you might find interesting: waving arms, a dripping faucet, yourself in a mirror, a spinning coin, ping pong games, a bouncing rubber ball, spinning bicycle wheels, a television show.

Start by turning the wheel very slowly, and then turn it faster. What happens? The slots in the wheel act as shutters that open and close, letting the light come through for only a fraction of a second at a time. The brighter the light, the more light will come through the shutter, and the brighter the image will be. A movie camera shutter works the same way. (Maybe someone will show you a camera shutter.)

The MOVIE WHEEL can also "show movies" by making a series of still pictures move. Draw a series of separate, sequential pictures, each between the slots on the wheel, ten pictures in all (see directions for making MOVIE WHEEL below). The pictures can be quite simple—a ball getting bigger, for example—or quite complicated. The three picture series in Fig. 1 will give you some ideas. Stand in front of a mirror and look through the slits while spinning the wheel. Be sure the drawing side of the wheel is facing the mirror and is well lit. The pictures will appear to move and come to life. Turn the wheel at different speeds. What do you see? What do you think might happen if you drew a series of nine or eleven pictures evenly spaced around the wheel? Try it.

| MATERIALS | TOOLS |
|-----------|-------|
| cardboard | pencil |
| | scissors |
| | ruler |
| | crayons |

## CONSTRUCTION

These instructions will show you how to make a simple cardboard MOVIE WHEEL. It is good for experimenting and will work fine, but it isn't very durable and you can't erase the drawings to do new ones. But before you decide to make the sturdier wooden version shown in Fig. 3, experiment first with the cardboard model. It is easy and quick to make.

Cut a cardboard circle about 8 to 12 inches round. Draw, then cut, ten slits in the edge of the wheel, Fig. 2. The slits should be as evenly spaced as you can figure them, and about 1/8 inch wide by 1 to 1 1/2 inches long. (Later you may want to experiment with these dimensions to see what happens.) Cut a finger hole in the center of the disc, and another hole an inch or two away for turning. Color the wheel a dark color with poster paint, color markers, or crayons (flat black is recommended). Remember that the MOVIE WHEEL works best in very bright light.

The wood version of the MOVIE WHEEL will require 1/4 inch plywood, 1/8 inch Masonite, or something similar. The entire disc should be painted flat black so pictures can be drawn with chalk and erased. Screw a wood dowel—long enough to hold onto easily—into one side of the wheel, through the center hole, Fig. 3. Use a wood screw and two flat washers, allowing the

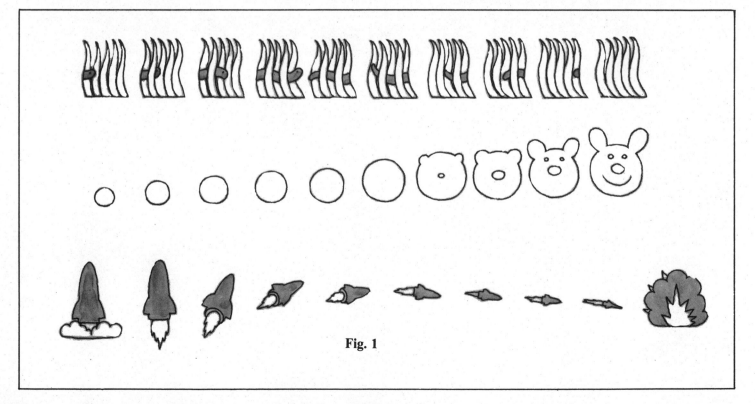

**Fig. 1**

47

wheel sufficient freedom to spin in place. The dowel acts as a permanent pivot.

## MAKING IT WORK

To work the cardboard MOVIE WHEEL, put your index finger, as if it were an axle, through the center hole from behind. From the front—the side facing you—place the index finger of the other hand through the off-center hole, and rotate the wheel as if you were dialing a telephone dial round and round.

The wooden wheel is worked similarly except that the dowel is held from behind while the wheel is spun with the finger from the front. The wheel moves, but the dowel remains stationary.

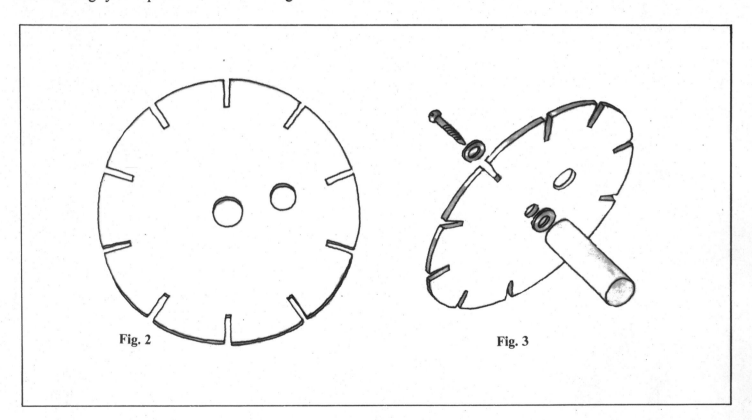

Fig. 2          Fig. 3

# Barometer

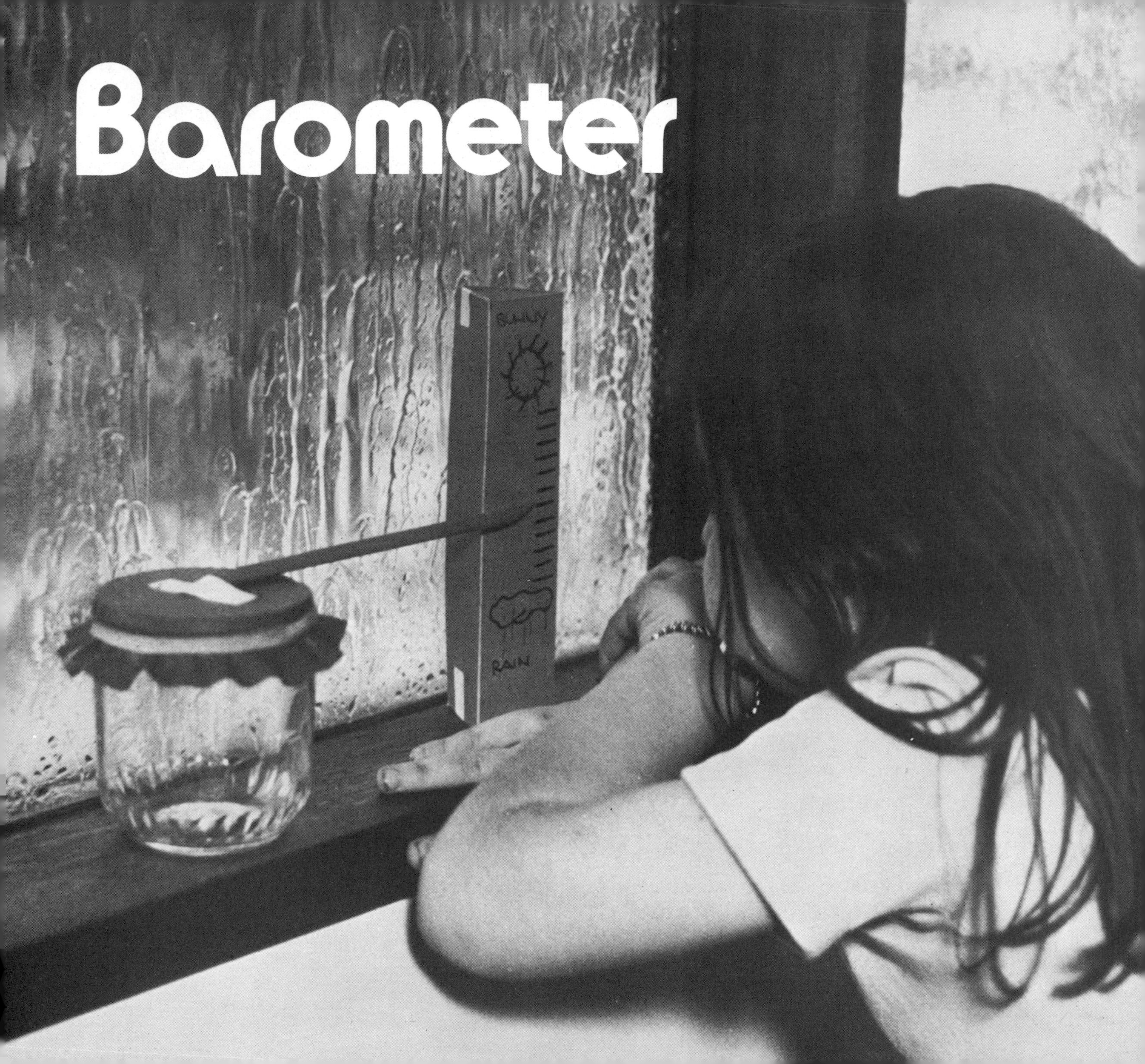

# Barometer

To predict a change in the weather, a weatherman needs to know the temperature, the wind direction, and what the weather is like in nearby and faraway places. But most important of all, he needs a BAROMETER to measure the air pressure—the force of the air pressing against the earth. Change in air pressure is one of the best predictors of the weather that's soon to arrive—rain, snow, wind, sun, or clouds. A BAROMETER will give you a clue to tomorrow's temperature too. If the air pressure goes up, the temperature will probably go down; if the air pressure goes down, the temperature probably will rise.

## MATERIALS

glass jar
balloon
rubber bands
drinking straw
tape
paper

## TOOLS

scissors
ruler
pencil

## CONSTRUCTION

Get a medium to large size glass jar with a wide mouth. Peanut butter jars are good. Wash out the jar and remove the label (you won't need the lid). Cut a piece of balloon large enough to fit over the mouth of the jar. Stretch the balloon smooth and tight, and hold it in place with one or two rubber bands around the top of the jar. The inside of the jar should now be airtight. "Point" the ends of a drinking straw by cutting them as shown in Fig. 1. With a small piece of tape, fasten one end of the straw to the center of the balloon. The BAROMETER is finished, but you will need a chart

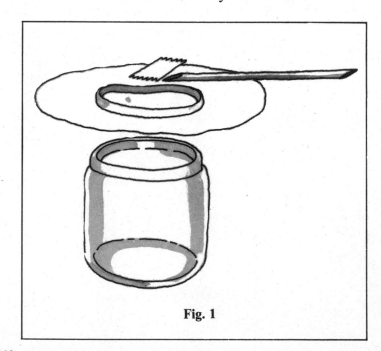

**Fig. 1**

to read the air pressure changes indicated by the movement of the pointer straw. Fold and tape a piece of paper into a triangular tube so that it will stand by itself and be a few inches taller than the jar, Fig. 2. Put the chart next to—but not touching—the pointer. Mark a small pencil line on the chart next to the tip of the pointer, and write the weather condition outside at that moment—stormy, rainy, cloudy, or sunny—opposite it. Check the position of the pointer once or twice a day to see if it has moved up or down. Each time it does move, put another line on the chart and write in the weather. After you have made some sunny and rainy marks on the chart, you will be able to predict the weather with reasonable accuracy. Just check in which direction the pointer is moving—towards sunny or stormy. To make certain that your predictions are as accurate as possible, you should put the BAROMETER in a place where the temperature doesn't change too much or too fast. (Don't put it on a radiator or by a window.) Can you figure out what makes the pointer move up or down? Look in a science book, or ask your teacher.

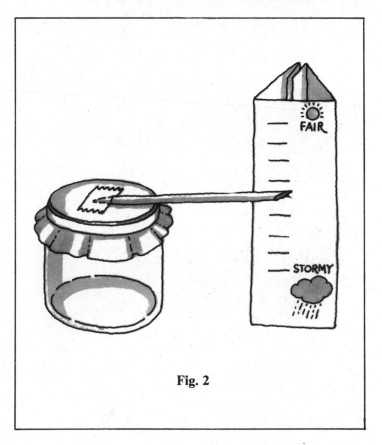

Fig. 2

Straw horn

# Straw horn

Some simple homemade toys, like classic jokes, seem to go on forever. Almost every kid learns how to make them, passing on their designs for yet another generation to acquire. The STRAW HORN could become such a standard. It all began with the advent of the plastic drinking straw.

By making a simple cut on one end of the straw, it becomes a real horn. The horn can be "tuned" to a different pitch by changing the length of the straw. The sound produced is a little strange—something between the moo of a cow, the screech of a crow, and the baa of a sheep. And like any good sound-maker, the STRAW HORN is loud. It's not exactly a musical instrument, but with two or more "horns" and players you can produce harmonies, even crude melodies. School cafeterias beware.

## MATERIALS

plastic drinking straw

## TOOLS

scissors

## CONSTRUCTION

Flatten out about 1 inch of the end of the drinking straw, and crease the sides well so that it stays fairly flat. With a scissors, trim the flattened end to a "V," as shown in the illustration. These become the horn reeds.

## PLAYING

Put the reed end of the straw in your mouth, just behind your lips, and blow hard. Does the horn work? Sometimes you have to experiment with making the reeds—lengthening or shortening them—and with holding them in your mouth. But it's all very easy to do. The shorter you cut the straw, the higher the sound, and the easier it is to blow.

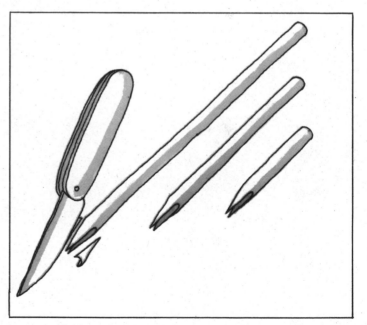

# Sundial

# Sundial

For thousands of years, man has devised some rather simple and ingenious ways of telling time. Clocks have been made using sand, rope, water, weights, candles, pendulums, motors, crystals, and many other interesting things. The first clock—the clock that cavemen might have used—was the sundial.

The sun's movement across the sky casts shadows from objects on the ground. By noting the position of the shadow during the day, you can determine the relative time of day. Every day is the same length, and the sun's movement is consistent and reliable.

But what do you do on cloudy days and dark nights when there are no sun shadows? To solve that problem, man kept on inventing better clocks. Sundials were still popular when the Pilgrims landed on Plymouth Rock, but today, except in some remote parts of the world, the sundial has given way to more modern clocks. Where it remains, it is used mostly for decoration.

There are actually hundreds of types of sundials, but almost anything that casts a shadow can be used for telling time. Just as there are different qualities of clocks and watches, there are different degrees of accuracy for sundials. Elaborate mathematical and astronomical calculations have been used to design accurate sundials, but here we are not so much concerned with precise accuracy as with simply building a sundial that works. The shadow stick is probably the simplest of sundials. Although a rather crude time-teller, it does work, and there is nothing technical you need to know. To make a shadow stick sundial, you'll need to locate an existing erect pole (telephone pole, flag-

pole, street light, tree, fence post, street sign). Or you can put a stick in the ground. There should be plenty of clearing around the pole so that buildings, trees, and other objects won't interfere with the sunlight. You should also consider your ability to see the pole easily when you choose its location.

There are formulas for calibrating a sundial to determine the placement of hour lines, but for the shadow stick we'll cheat a little. You can mark off the hours with the help of a wristwatch or house clock. Start early in the morning, as soon as the sun rises. Every hour on the hour, place a marker at the tip of the shadow from the pole. If the pole is very tall and the shadow very long, put the marker on the shadow line. The best shadow sticks are only a few feet high, with the markers placed at the shadow's tip. If you miss a few hours during the day, you can fill them in on later days. Markers can be made by using wood stakes and house numbers corresponding to the hour; see the illustration. Use paint or crayon for marking on asphalt or concrete. Chalk is good for experimenting, but it washes away with the rain. Remember that your sundial is being set for either standard or daylight saving time, so you'll have to change the markers at some point.

Test the accuracy of the shadow stick—is it still telling correct time after a week, month, winter, summer? Do you think a moondial would work?

Waterscope

# Water scope

There is a mysterious world under the water which remains hidden by the light reflections on the water's surface. Even if you try looking straight down into the water, the little you do see is often blurred. The WATER SCOPE eliminates the reflections to reveal the sights below the water's surface. Depending on what's down there, you may be able to see fish and other sea creatures, plant life, rocks, maybe even sunken treasure.

The WATER SCOPE will work in any body of water—pond, ocean, lake, river, or bathtub—but if the water is cloudy or choked with algae, you may not be able to see anything. (In this case, you should delay building the WATER SCOPE and write a letter to your congressman, complaining about water pollution.)

The WATER SCOPE is also an underwater magnifier that will make things at the sea bottom appear larger. As you put the scope in the water, the water pressure causes the clear plastic to push up, forming a magnifying lens. The deeper you put the scope, the stronger the water pressure, and the more powerful the magnification. (This magnifying principle is very similar to the one for the WATER LENS elsewhere in this book.) Never put the water scope completely below the water surface, or it will fill with water and not work. If water does get inside the scope, pour it out.

## MATERIALS

small plastic bucket
plastic wrap
elastic

## TOOLS

penknife
scissors

## CONSTRUCTION

Any small plastic bucket will do. You can also

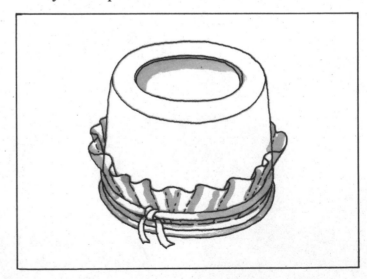

WATER SCOPE AND MAGNIFIER

use a plastic jug or a tin can with both ends cut out. Cutting carefully with a penknife, remove a big circle from the bottom of the bucket. Cut a piece of clear plastic food wrap or clear plastic clothes wrap from the cleaner's—it should be large enough to cover the top of the bucket. Se-cure the plastic in place over the bucket with a big rubber band or piece of elastic; see the illustration. If you're using a plastic jug, cover the cut-out hole on the bottom. The elastic must be tight to keep the water from leaking in.

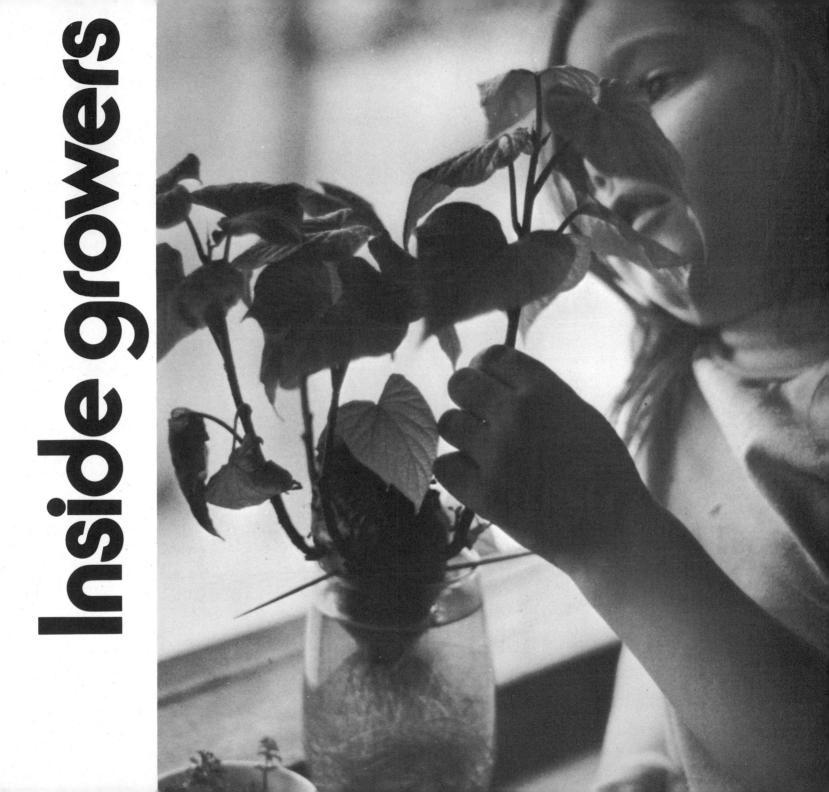

Inside growers

# Inside growers

Planting seeds is one of the easiest things you'll ever do. Even a three-year-old enjoys poking a finger in the soil and dropping in a seed. But the real excitement is when the seed cracks open and the sprout begins to grow up towards the light. The root descends, and the seed itself gets smaller and smaller until it finally disappears. Usually all this takes place under the soil. That's unfortunate. But INSIDE GROWERS are designed to let you see the complete process, all year round.

Almost any seed will grow if you know how to plant it, but often the process takes a long time, and you may get impatient. That's why it's good to be able to watch the germination of the seed and the growing process from the beginning. Remember, though, that planting and caring for growing things does take attention, and should probably be a joint family responsibility. You don't need to keep charts and records; just the fun of doing and watching is learning enough. A bit of life's explanation will become apparent— from the sprouting of the seed to the withering of the flower.

Since the growing *process* is what seems to be most interesting, it's not terribly important what you grow. All seeds need water and air. Too much water and not enough air can cause the seeds to drown, so keep the seeds moist, but don't overwater. Room temperature is the perfect temperature for seed growing.

**Water Jar and Toothpicks**

Things to grow: sweet potato, beet, onion, or garlic.

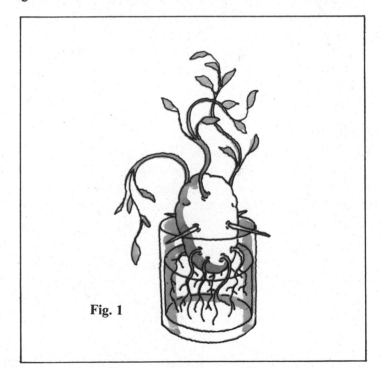

Fig. 1

Stick three or four toothpicks around the middle of the vegetable to suspend it in the mouth of a glass jar. The jar should be large enough not to cramp future roots. Fill the jar with water so that the bottom part of the vegetable is covered, Fig. 1. Check the water every few days and fill the jar back up to the proper level. Keep the jar on a sunny window. It takes about two weeks for a vine to start growing.

### Wet Paper Towels

Things to grow: lentil beans, watercress seeds, string bean seeds and most common fruit seeds.

Line the bottom of a dish, cake pan, or shallow pot with six to ten layers of paper towels. Water the paper until it is thoroughly wet, but without water puddles. Place the seeds on top of the towels, Fig. 2. Be sure the paper stays moist, and keep the grower on a sunny window. Lentil and cress will begin to grow in less than a week.

### Water Dish

Things to grow: carrot tops, pineapple tops, turnip tops.

Take a 1-inch slice off the top of the fruit, and place it in a shallow dish of water, Fig. 3. Keep it on a sunny window, but don't let the water dry out. In about one week new shoots will start to grow.

### Sponge and Glass

Things to grow: lima beans, corn, grapefruit seeds, lemon seeds, kidney beans, apple seeds, sweet peas, orange seeds, squash seeds, pear seeds, and many, many others.

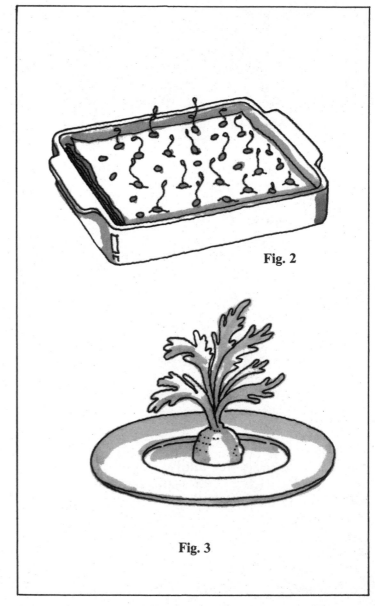

Fig. 2

Fig. 3

Place a sponge around the inside of a clear drinking glass or jar. Pour a little water in the bottom of the glass, but not so much that the sponge becomes soaking wet. Place a few seeds between the glass jar and sponge, Fig. 4. You can mix different kinds of seeds. The sponge should be kept moist, and the jar placed on a sunny window.

INSIDE GROWERS are to start seeds growing. You can leave some seedlings in the growers to see what will happen to them there, but also try transplanting a few in potting soil. An empty egg carton makes a good planter.

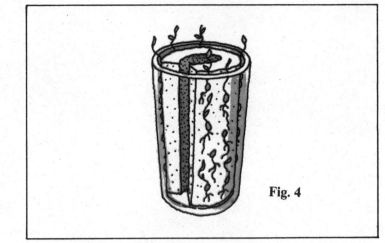

Fig. 4

# Curds and whey

# Curds and whey

Little Miss Muffet sat on a tuffet eating her cottage cheese. That's right. Curds is the cottage cheese and whey is the liquid by-product you get when making curds. Cottage cheese is quite simple to make, and a good project for learning how to cook. The ingredients are common, and the results are fast and spectacular. What's more, you'll have only a few pots and things to clean up. The cottage cheese tastes quite good, though you might want to add a little salt for taste, or sour cream for smoothness. If there is any cheese left over, keep it in the refrigerator.

## INGREDIENTS

2 cups whole milk, or
   milk that has been
   soured
1 tablespoon vinegar

## UTENSILS

cooking pot or
   saucepan
mixing spoon
strainer
bowl

## RECIPE

Pour two cups of milk in the pot, and cook at medium heat until bubbles begin to form on the top. Stir while heating. Remove the pot from the heat and stir in a tablespoon of vinegar. Keep stirring gently, and look for the curds to form. It happens quickly so keep your eyes on the pot. The liquid left over is the whey.

Stir a few times while the mixture cools, and then pour off the whey through a strainer, keeping the curds; see the illustration. Gently squeeze the curds with the mixing spoon to be sure all the whey is removed. Now go ahead and taste it.

# Creature cage

# Creature cage

Did you ever see a bug creature up close? Most grown-ups would much rather do their looking from a distance, but kids like to catch the creature and confine him temporarily for close observation. That's fine, but too often the confinement takes place inside a mayonaise jar with a perforated lid. The bug may be safe inside, but a kid chasing after a butterfly while clutching the glass jar might not be. And maybe the bug is safe, but is he really happy? It gets pretty hot and damp inside a jar, and sometimes it's difficult to climb glass walls.

The CREATURE CAGE comes a little closer to the bug's natural environment—especially if you add a few leaves and grass. The cage is secure, yet well ventilated, and its caps will easily and quickly slip on and off. Take a good close look at the caught creature, then let him go in time for his next meal.

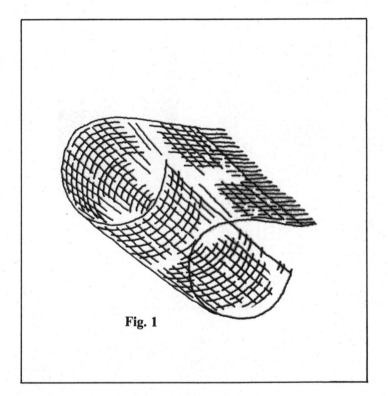

**Fig. 1**

## MATERIALS

2 empty tuna cans
wire screen

## TOOLS

scissors

## CONSTRUCTION

Save two identical tuna cans, removing lids and labels (these may be soaked off in hot water).

Pineapple ring cans work well also. Check to be sure that there are no sharp edges, then wash the cans thoroughly. Cut a length of wire screen about 6 inches wide and long enough to go around the inside of the can, plus an inch, Fig. 1.

Wire screen cuts easily with a scissors. Bend the screen into a tube to fit the inside size of the cans. Fasten the screen in that shape by first stripping a few wire strands from the outside overlap edge and bending the exposed row of wire prongs inward. Then fit the prongs through the inside screen, bending the prongs over and shut, Fig. 2. Fit the cans over each end of the screen tube to complete the bugproof CREATURE CAGE, Fig. 3.

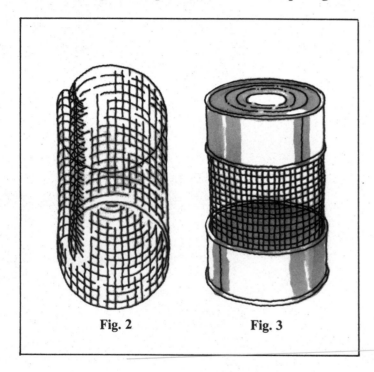

Fig. 2          Fig. 3

# PRETENDING TOYS

# Tube telephone

# Tube telephone

Tube telephones were once actually used in big ships so the captain could talk to the engine room and other parts of the boat. Somehow being able to talk with a friend you cannot see is exciting—it's your own private line for secret messages. Even when you talk softly into one end of the TUBE TELEPHONE, the person at the other end will hear you loud and clear. You can hook up the phone system anywhere—from one room to another, down the hall, around the corner, upstairs to downstairs, even to another house or apartment. After you discover how well they work, think about what would happen if the Telephone Company used nothing but TUBE TELEPHONES.

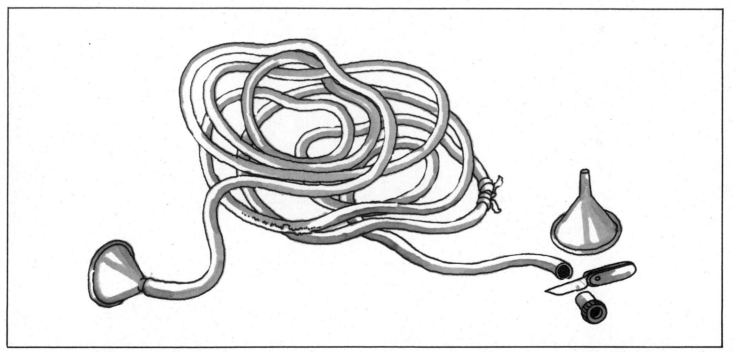

# TUBE TELEPHONE

## MATERIALS

old garden hose
2 plastic funnels, about
   4 inches in diameter

## TOOLS

penknife

## CONSTRUCTION

Try to find an old, ready-to-be-discarded garden hose, and tape up any holes or cuts. If you must buy a new hose, get the cheapest one you can—it will work fine. Hoses usually come in 25- and 50-foot lengths. You can make a TUBE TELEPHONE as long or as short as you want by using one hose or putting two or more together. Cut the metal couplings off the ends of the length of hose, and push a funnel into each end; see illustration. Now you are ready to "hook up the line," so find someone to talk with, and pick two places to talk from. The TUBE TELEPHONE doesn't have to be straight; it can make as many twists and curves as you want, but do be sure the hose doesn't get bent closed, which will stop the sound from traveling through. While one person talks into one end of the phone, the person at the other end listens by holding the funnel up close to an ear. Invent code signals, like saying the word "over" when you are finished talking and want a reply. If you get very ambitious, you can make branch lines by adding one or more "Y" hose connectors and some more hoses. This way you can have three- or four-way conversations. The next time you see a big shipping box—the kind a refrigerator, stove or washing machine comes in—you might try making a telephone booth for a little more privacy.

# Pretend play cutouts

# Pretend play cutouts

Maybe there are things you'd like to do, but you can't because you're not "big enough." Well, you can—if you let yourself do a little pretending. It's fun to talk and act like grown-ups, and the more like them you can be, the better it feels. (You can run things the way you want when you're making believe.) Most pretend play takes place in your head, but you need a few props to get it all going and, of course, to make it real.

PRETEND PLAY CUTOUTS let you create your own make-believe world, complete with houses, furniture, people, pets, cars, trucks, trees, factories—almost anything you like.

MATERIALS

old magazines
cardboard
paper glue or paste

TOOLS

scissors

Fig. 1

Fig. 2

Fig. 3

## CONSTRUCTION

Gather together a bunch of old magazines, catalogs, and junk mail. (Mail-order catalogs are especially good.) Look for pictures of people and things you'd like to use for pretend play, and cut them out. Don't try to follow the exact shape of the object—it's really not necessary. If you want to add more realism, you can try to match everything to scale. For example, say 1 foot of a real object equals 1 inch of a cutout. Then you would have to find a man cutout about 6 inches tall, a child about 3 or 4 inches tall, and so on. Paste all the cutouts on thin cardboard (from shirts, shoe boxes, or paper pad backs) and patiently wait until the glue dries, Fig. 1. With a good sharp scissors, cut out the shapes again, but this time try to stay a little closer to the outline, and be certain to make a straight-across cut at the bottom, Fig. 2. Using the scrap cardboard leftovers, make small triangular stands, again being sure to cut straight across the bottom, Fig. 2. Cut a short slit in the center bottom of each cutout, and a short slit in the center top of the stands. Fit the slits of the stand and cutout together so that the bottom of both are flush and the PRETEND PLAY CUTOUT will stand by itself, Fig. 3. You can keep adding to your cutout collection and create an entire family, fill a doll house, or build a village—whatever you want to pretend.

Soap floats

# Soap floats

Taking a bath should be one of the best events of the day—a ready-made space for water play. But some parents tend to rush the bath process. Baths are for getting clean, but there's also the feel of the water, the sounds it makes when splashed, and the way things float on it. Water is a great source of play—it's cheap, almost always available, and doesn't have to be stored. So before getting down to the business of washing up, kids should have a little soak-time to play with sponges, soft plastic squeeze bottles, and SOAP FLOATS. SOAP FLOATS can be most any shape that will stick into a bar of floating soap— sailboat, water skier, seaplane, or barge—but water creatures somehow seem most appropriate:

| hippo | duck | shark |
| octopus | sea horse | lobster |
| spider | whale | lizzard |
| frog | starfish | Loch Ness Monster |
| beaver | stingray | alligator |
| turtle | snail | jellyfish |

## MATERIALS

soft plastic (see below)
Ivory Soap bar

## TOOLS

ball-point pen
scissors or knife

## CONSTRUCTION

Pieces of thin soft plastic are more common than you may think—lids of coffee cans, ice cream containers, discarded wastepaper baskets, and many types of plastic wash pans and tubs. An Ivory Soap bar (big or little size) works be-

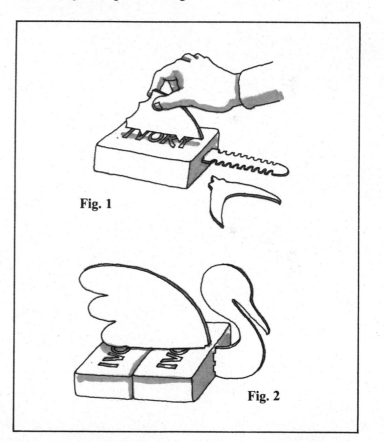

Fig. 1

Fig. 2

cause it floats, and is soft enough to stick the plastic into. From the suggestions and designs in Fig. 2, pick a creature to make, and draw it out on the plastic piece you've found. A ball-point pen will write best on soft plastic. Remember to keep the drawing in scale with the bar of soap. You can think of the soap bar as the creature's body. Add small wedges to the design that will stick and hold in the soap. One hint—it's best not to build too high, or the floating creature might tip over. With a big scissors or penknife, cut out the plastic shapes. Cutting plastic is probably too tough for most kids, so get help from someone older. Push the wedges into the soap bar to make your SOAP FLOAT creature, Fig. 1. You might

have to shift the plastic parts around so the soap bar balances, or maybe add a few extra parts. But creatures are supposed to look a little strange.

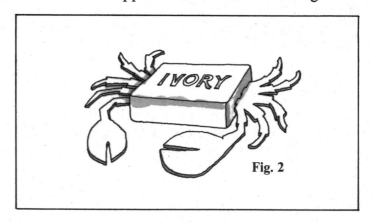

Fig. 2

# Sand combs

# Sand combs

Sand can be a great friend. Combine it with a pail of water, a few stones, shells, and small cars, and you can have a glorious sand world. SAND COMBS make textures that can become roadways, rivers, castles, bridges, railroads, farm fields, airports, canals, or whatever else you want to imagine. With a little help from your friends, you can have a whole village. Maybe each person can be in charge of a specific job—the river maker and the road maker, for example. If you have rivers and roads that meet, you better have a bridge builder as well.

MATERIALS

thin wood (or
    hardboard, plywood,
    heavy cardboard)

TOOLS

coping saw
ruler
pencil

CONSTRUCTION

Find, or cut, a piece of thin wood—about 1/4 inch thick or less—to about 4 by 8 inches. The exact size or shape is not important, so you can make it a little larger or smaller to fit the material you have. Pick two sand comb teeth patterns from the ones illustrated, and draw your own freehand version of the patterns, one on each long side of the piece of wood. Carefully cut out the pattern shapes with a coping saw. It's that simple. Now find some sand, and start combing. Later you can invent your own sand comb patterns.

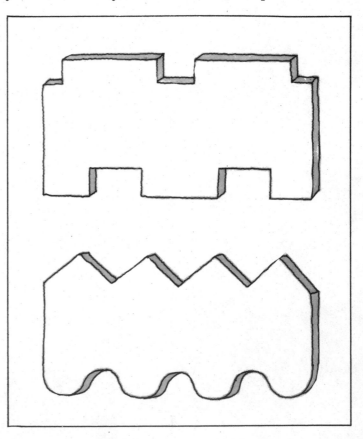

Moustaches

# Moustaches

There is probably no other disguise that can change a person's appearance so quickly as a fine moustache. Behind a moustache you can be any-body—politician, playboy, detective, television star, or even the bearded circus lady. Dressing up is great fun, and every kid should have a special drawer or dress-up box of old shoes, out-of-style hats, dresses, jewelry—and moustaches. Actually, a moustache can be the whole costume, as most of the time you really don't need an elaborate disguise. Still, if you think that the moustache alone isn't convincing, a large bath towel and a few diaper pins can help round out your image. It's fun to imitate life—being the "baddy," with a

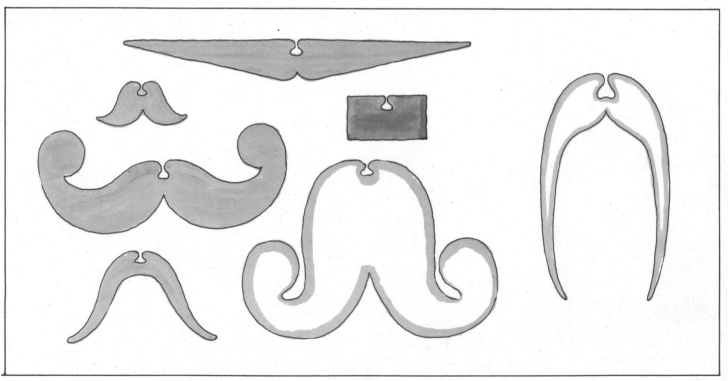

pencil-thin moustache curled up at the end, or maybe the "goody," with a big floppy moustache. You won't really feel the magic of your moustache disguise until you see yourself in a mirror. Then—wow.

## MATERIALS

heavy paper

## TOOLS

pencil
scissors

## CONSTRUCTION

The moustaches shown in the illustrations are only examples. You can try to copy them, or make up your own. It's easy to invent a moustache. Draw the moustache pattern on a sheet of heavy paper—like construction paper, old postcards, or file folders. Cut out the moustache with scissors, and try it on for size. Be sure to make the two little hook cutouts that attach to your nose. Experiment until you get the hooks just right so the moustache will stay in place. That's all there is to it. Now why not have a moustache party or maybe a moustache day.

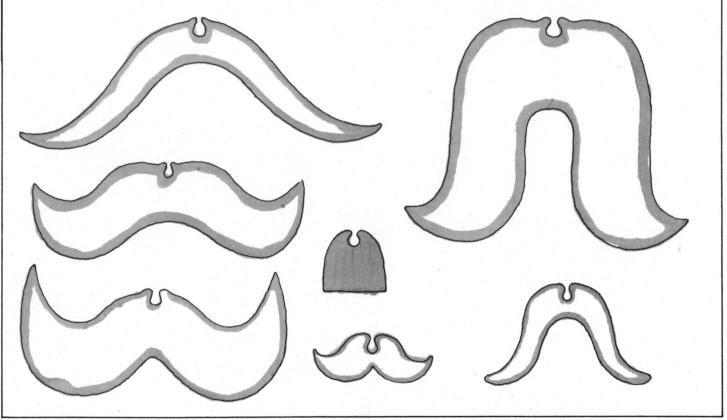

# GAMES

# Substitution

# Substitution
## (for parents also)

Most card games are designed for a specific age group—simple games of guess and chance for young players, games of skill and strategy for older kids and adults. Here's a rare find. A solitaire game that's fun and easy for a six-year-old, yet intellectually stimulating (and sometimes quite difficult) even for "Einsteins." More good news. It takes only a few minutes to make, and about the same time to learn the rules.

MATERIALS      TOOLS

paper                    scissors
pencil (or crayon)

CONSTRUCTION

Cut about twenty small squares of paper. The exact size and quantity are unimportant—you might try cutting an index card in two. On half the cards draw a circle symbol, and on the remaining cards draw a square symbol. For easy recognition, especially if kids are playing, it's a good idea to give each symbol its own color—making, for example, all circles blue and all squares red. These are the game cards; now make the rule cards. Cut about ten larger strips of paper or use uncut index cards. On each of the strips write a circle and square equation. Here are some examples chosen from the total number of possible permutations. Use these, or any of the other possibilities:

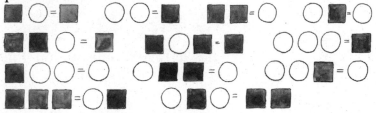

HOW TO PLAY

1) Shuffle the game cards.
2) Lay out all the game cards in a row, face up, in their shuffled order. We've chosen to use fourteen cards:

■○○■○■■■○■○○■○

3) Shuffle the rule cards, pick the top two, and place them below the row of game cards, face up:

game cards:

■○○■○■■■○■○○■○

rule cards:

■○=○                 ○■○=■

4) The object of the game is to use the substitu-

tion equations of the two rule cards to reduce the row of game cards to as few as possible. A single card remaining is the best you can do.

Here's an example of playing the game, using the card set-up which appears above.

1st play: Acting upon the substitution equation of the left-hand rule card, the player removes ▪ ● cards and substitutes a ● card:

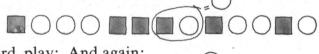

2nd play: Using the left-hand substitution rule again:

3rd play: And again:

4th play: Now acting upon the right-hand substitution rule card:

5th play: Using the right-hand substitution rule again:

6th play: Now the left-hand:

7th play: Now the right:

8th play: Now the left again:

End of the game—no more substitutions can be made. Too bad, we're left with three cards:

Obviously, any specific combination of game and rule cards can have many different solutions, and the length of the starting line to some degree determines difficulty. A sophisticated player will plan strategies many moves ahead. If you want even more of a challenge, here are a few game variations:

Same game, but this time you're allowed to use the rule cards in reverse also—that is, you can use the equations to lengthen as well as shorten the row. The object is still to end up with the shortest row.

Start with a single game card and two rule cards. Try to lengthen the row to use all the game cards.

As a competitive game, have two or more players, each with identical starting rows and rule cards. See who does best.

Hexaflexagon

# Hexaflexagon

A hard word to say, but an easy-to-make hand puzzle that flips and twists inside out to create many different color-pattern combinations. HEXAFLEXAGON is a puzzle that helps stretch your mind. It's quite simple, yet challenging. You can just fidget with it, or work out a strategy to discover all the possible pattern combinations. You can play with it by yourself, or invent games—like daring someone to make a particular pattern.

## MATERIALS

stiff paper
glue
crayons

## TOOLS

pencil
ruler
scissors
60-degree angle

## CONSTRUCTION

Find a plain piece of stiff paper. Here are some suggestions: construction paper, file folders, manila envelopes, heavy wrapping paper. Cut a strip of the paper about 2 inches wide and 14 inches long. The size does not have to be exact, and you can try making the HEXAFLEXAGON larger or smaller proportionately. Using a 60-degree angle and a pencil, mark off ten equilateral triangles on the strip, Fig. 1. If you don't have a 60-degree angle, trace the one in Fig. 1, and then cut out the tracing. Press down hard with the pencil to score the paper. "Score" means to put a slight indentation in the paper, making it easy to fold on the drawn line. Cut off the excess at both ends of the

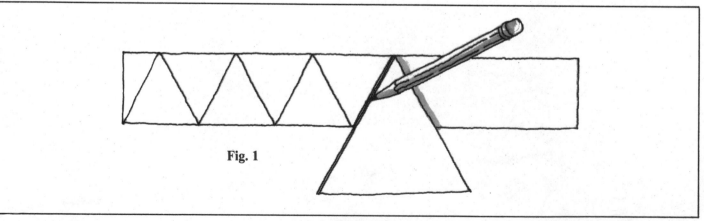

**Fig. 1**

strip so that you now have just a strip of ten triangles, Fig. 2. Fold each triangle back and forth on the score line, and then lay the strip out flat again, Fig. 3. Fold the strip over and over—always in the same direction—as shown in Fig. 4. The shape of the folded piece should be a hexagon (6 sides). Glue together the two ends that meet, Fig. 5, and wait until the glue dries before going further. Color each side of the folded HEX-AFLEXAGON a different color, using crayons, water paint, or color markers. Open up the HEX-AFLEXAGON by gently twisting it on the folds, until it goes flat again into another hexagon—but this time you should get a combination of colors on each side, including the plain paper color. How many different patterns do you think can be made? Can you flip the HEXAFLEXAGON to make one side all the plain paper color? Once you get the knack of it, try making another HEXA-FLEXAGON, but now use many different colors to fill in the triangles.

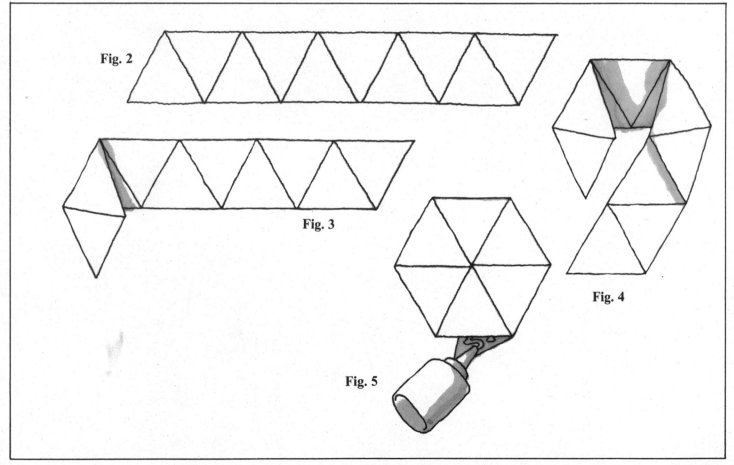

Fig. 2

Fig. 3

Fig. 4

Fig. 5

# Great turtle race

# Great turtle race

Kids like to play competitive games—as long as the spirit of fun always comes first. A game is the chance to measure your abilities against others', to let off steam, and to exercise your alertness. The GREAT TURTLE RACE is a game of skill, but an equal challenge to everyone in the family. It's impossible to resist playing, and kids seem to have a special knack for winning. The game is especially appropriate for parties or rainy day fun.

## MATERIALS

stiff cardboard
string

## TOOLS

pencil
scissors
crayons

## CONSTRUCTION

If you're going to have a race, make two or more turtles, but first practice by making one. Find a piece of stiff cardboard about 10 or 12

inches high. Some materials that work well are shirt, gift or shoe box cardboard, the back of a paper pad, or a corrugated box. Draw a turtle-shape pattern on the cardboard. It's not important that the turtle be the exact shape of the one in the illustration, but be certain that the rear legs go below the body and tail. Cut out the turtle shape, and punch a hole through the cardboard a little below the turtle's head. The hole should be about as big around as a pencil (so you might use a pencil to punch the hole). Decorate the turtle by drawing the head, eyes, legs, and shell pattern on *both* sides. Cut a piece of string about 10 feet long—you can experiment later with longer or shorter pieces of string. Tie one end of the string to a chair or table leg at about the same height as the turtle is tall. Thread the other end of the string through the hole in the turtle. Now you're ready to practice racing. Hold the loose end of the string in your hand and pull it taut. By slackening the string slightly, and then giving it a small jerk, you can make the turtle "walk." Remember that it does take some practice to get it just right. When the turtle gets to either end of the string, jerk the string up slightly, and the turtle will flip over and be ready to race back. Now you can make some more turtles and have races. Before a race, it's a good idea to agree on the start and finish lines, and the number of laps. Although the turtle can race much faster on rough or carpeted floors, the racing becomes much more difficult and challenging on a smooth floor. Instead of drawing a turtle pattern, you might want to invent other racers, like a car, rabbit, boat, person, airplane, dog, horse, or whatever.

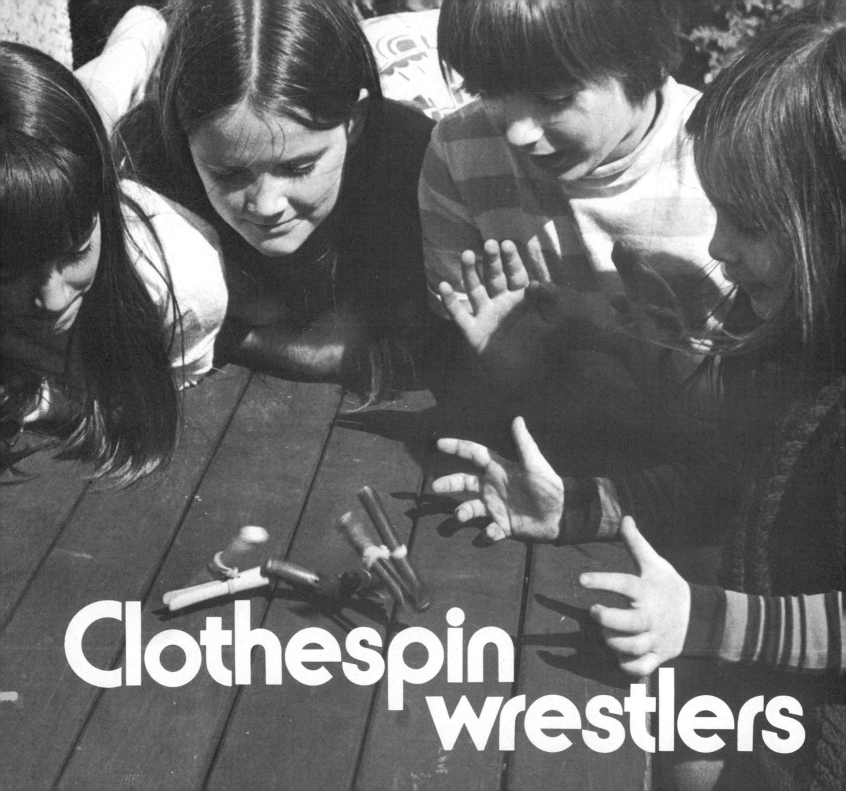

# Clothespin
# wrestlers

# Clothespin wrestlers

Place your bets. Wind up the wrestlers—not too tight—and carefully put them down. Now quickly let go. For a few seconds the wrestlers will knock each other all over the place, but in the end, one wrestler will land on top of the other and be the winner. Sometimes neither wrestler will win. Is it a game of chance or a game of skill? Can you predict which wrestler will win? Does it make any difference how much you wind up the wrestlers or the way you put them down? Play is the process of finding out. You might try having clothespin wrestling contests, with winners playing winners. Maybe you know how to make a champion wrestler.

## MATERIALS

2 clothespins
fat rubber band

## CONSTRUCTION

Decorate each of the clothespins a different color, with the meanest looking faces you can draw. Round wood clothespins work best. Look carefully at the illustration, and hook the rubber band around both clothespins as shown. Now you're ready to wrestle.

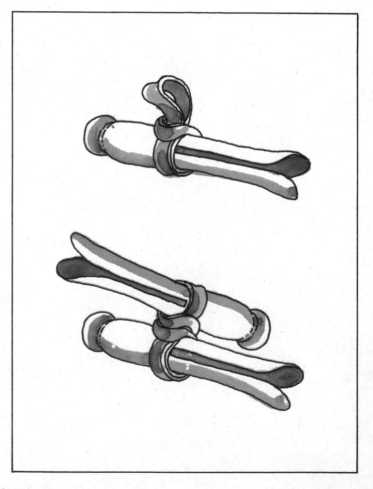

# Racing spools

# Racing spools

A RACING SPOOL is really supersimple to make. But if you want to have the fastest, or the best looking, or the racer that will go the longest distance, you'll have to do some experimenting—and that's all the fun. Somehow you can't build just one. The challenges of competition are too great.

MATERIALS          TOOLS
large wooden spool     hammer
rubber band
carpet tack
short stick
flat washer

## CONSTRUCTION

Hammer the carpet tack into one side of the spool, but not all the way—let the head of the tack stick out just a little. Cut a small stick or twig to about 4 or 5 inches long. A short pencil will also do, but play it safe and break off the pencil point so no one will get stuck. Push the rubber band through the hole in the center of the spool (sometimes pushing with a toothpick helps) and loop one end around the tack. Ideally, the rubber band should just stick out the other end of the spool. If it is much too long, you can double it up, tie a knot to shorten it, or try to find a shorter

rubber band. Slip the flat washer over the free end of the rubber band, and then push the stick about 1 inch through the rubber band loop. You're now ready for the first test race. Hold the RACING SPOOL in one hand, and wind up the stick. When you think that the rubber band is wound tightly enough, carefully put the racer on the floor (still holding onto the stick), take aim, and let go. Zap! If you've built a good racer, it will shoot straight across the floor. Even so, you might want

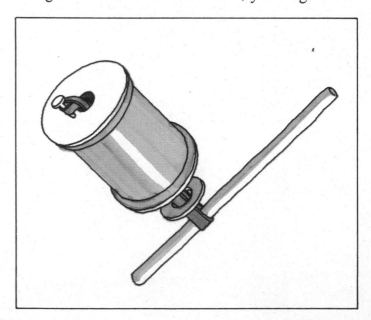

to experiment a little. Try winding up the stick a little less—and then a little more. Use a fat rubber band, a skinny rubber band, and maybe two or three rubber bands together. Try racing the spool on a smooth floor, on a rug, or on the grass. Do you think that the racer would work any better if you cut some notches around the edge of the spool? When you have finally made a champion racer, give it a fancy paint job—with a little water color or color marker—and maybe even a racing number. There are many different kinds of spool races—long distance, steep hill climb, obstacle course, or first to cross the finish line. But you make up the rules—kids are good at that.

# Ring and pin

# Ring and pin

American Indians have invented some pretty interesting games. RING AND PIN was a gambling game played by Indian women, but their kids couldn't resist trying it, just for fun. There are now more than a hundred versions of RING AND PIN from all over the world, but the way to play the game is always the same—to see how many rings you can catch on the stick.

| MATERIALS | TOOLS |
|---|---|
| rings (see below) | penknife |
| stick | |
| heavy string | |

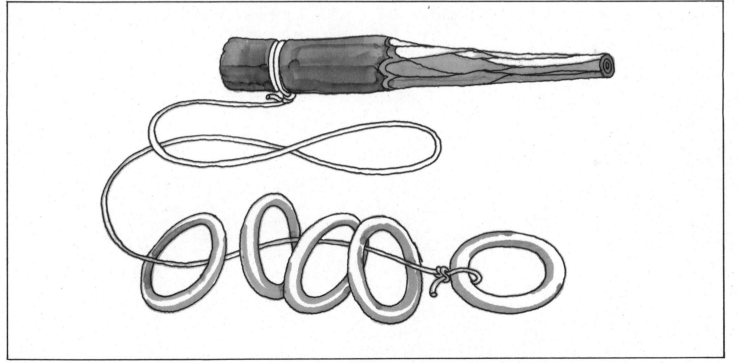

## CONSTRUCTION

Look around the house to find six to eight rings all about the same size—about 2 to 4 inches across. Here are some suggestions: wooden curtain rings; rings cut from a heavy paper tube or plastic drinking cup; rings sliced 3/4 inch thick from a dried gourd or squash; rings sawed from a dried marrow ("pin") bone. Gourds and marrow bones make the best rings, but both require drying, and can be difficult to cut. Ask the butcher for a marrow bone, and he might even slice it up in rings for you on his electric saw. Find a stick about 10 or 12 inches long, and carve one end of it down to a dull point, using a penknife; see the illustration. Be sure the sharp edge of the penknife blade points away from you while carving. Cut a piece of heavy string or twine about 3 feet long, or tie a couple of shoe laces together. (If you want to be authentic, use a piece of leather thong.) Tie one end of the string to the fat end of the stick—a small whittled groove will keep the string from slipping off. Thread all but one of the rings onto the string, and then tie the remaining ring to the free end of the string. If all the rings are not the same size, the tied-on ring should be the biggest.

## PLAYING

Hold the fat end of the stick in your hand, with the rings hanging down. Flip or swing the rings up, trying to catch as many as you can with the pointed end of the stick. Remember, you're doing this all with one hand, and it takes practice to get really good.

You can make up your own rules for keeping score, but here are some to start with. Each ring you catch is worth one point. Players take turns, and the first one to score a total of twenty points is the winner.

# Number square

# Number square

Pencil-and-paper games have always meant something to do when there's nothing to do, and the NUMBER SQUARE PUZZLE is just this sort of fun. This is a simple game of skill that any number or age can play—or may be enjoyed all by yourself. For a preschooler, the puzzle is a great way to help learn number recognition, counting, and maybe even the satisfaction of competition. But winning should never be your objective, or you might forget to have fun. The larger you make the puzzle, the more difficult it is to win, and an older kid will probably discover the need to look ahead a few moves to plan a strategy. Playing the game takes only a few minutes, so keep a score sheet to see who wins the most games. If you're playing by yourself, try to do the game in the fewest number of moves.

## MATERIALS

paper
pencil
markers (peas, buttons, pebbles, etc.)

## CONSTRUCTION

Draw horizontal and vertical lines on a regular size sheet of paper to make a gridwork of boxes.

Remember, the more boxes you draw, the more difficult the game. A simple grid might have 289 boxes (18 lines across and 18 lines down). If you have graph paper, the boxes are already drawn, and you can outline the number of squares you want to use. Fill in every box on the grid with a number from 0 to 9, as in the illustration. Make the number placement as random as possible, but only one number to a box. Find the middle square (it should not be a 0), and draw a circle around it.

## HOW TO PLAY

The object of the game is to see who can land *just outside* the game grid on his *last move*. That is, the player tries to discover a number path which will bring him outside the grid by the exact count of the numbers on which he lands. The illustration shows the moves made by three players. One player has already won, which of the other players do you think will come in second? Every player starts at the middle square. Small markers are used to indicate a player's position. Turns are taken one at a time and in order. Each player gets to move the number of boxes indicated by the number in the square he lands on; that is, the number on which he lands indicates the number he can move on his next turn. Moves can be made in any direction—up, down, across, or diagonally—but you cannot change direction during·a move. For each game you make, you'll soon learn a few quick paths to get out of the grid and win—especially if you've made a simple game. So it's a good idea to make many different game grids and use them alternately.

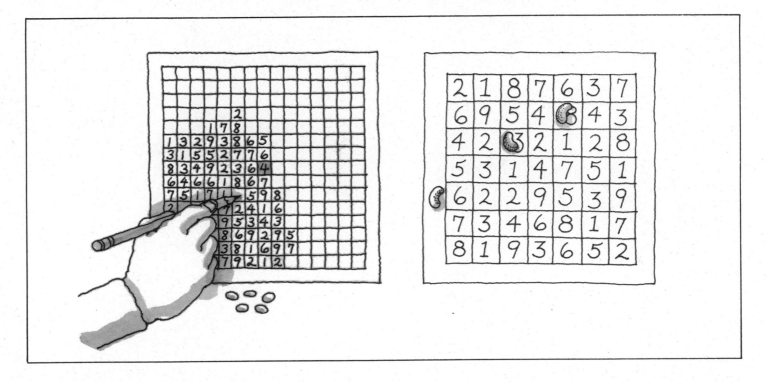

# BUILDING TOYS

# Building circles

# Building circles

BUILDING CIRCLES is a modular construction toy. The pieces fit together in any direction, and there are no rules as to what you can make. With a batch of folded paper plates and some rubber bands, you can build hundreds of different forms and patterns—towers, globes, hats, mobiles, or whatever. The circles are easily connected with rubber bands, and they come apart easily to be used over and over again.

| MATERIALS | TOOLS |
|---|---|
| round paper plates | pencil |
| rubber bands | straight edge |
| | paper hole punch |
| | 60-degree angle |

## CONSTRUCTION

You can use any size round paper plate, but 6-inch plates are easy to work with, and the least expensive. A package of one hundred plates should be plenty to do many different constructions. The rubber bands should be about half the diameter of the plates, or a little less (for the 6-inch plates, a thin 2 1/2-inch rubber band works best). In order to draw the folding pattern on the paper plates, you first need to make a triangle template. A template is a guide you can use to trace the folding pattern in exactly the same way on all the plates. To make the template, use a 60-degree angle. Place the 60-degree angle on one paper plate (that you have flattened out a little), making sure that the point of the angle just touches the edge of the plate. Make a pencil mark at that point. Make a pencil mark where each of the other two arms of the triangle touch the edge

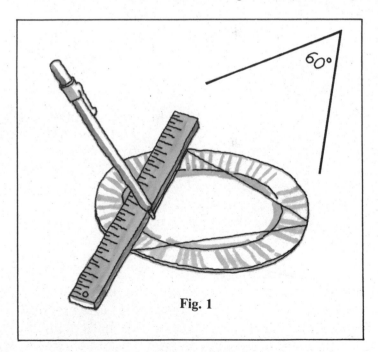

**Fig. 1**

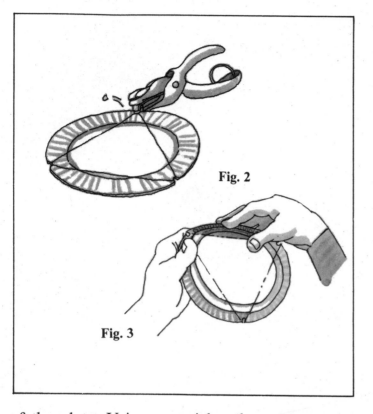

Fig. 2

Fig. 3

pencil (or ball-point pen) when making the lines to score the paper. ("Score" means to put a slight indentation in the paper to make it easy to fold on the drawn line.) With a paper hole punch, put three notches in the edge of each plate at the triangle points, Fig. 2. Fold the three flaps on the scored lines of the triangle. Flaps must be folded backwards (towards the underside of the plate), Fig. 3. That helps to flatten the plate. Do the same thing to all the paper plates. To connect the BUILDING CIRCLES, start with two circle parts, and put a flap from each together. Now stretch a rubber band around the flaps, making sure it hooks into the notches, Fig. 3. Keep adding circles by connecting flaps together. The BUILDING CIRCLES can be decorated with color or cutouts in the center of the circles. As with any toy that has a lot of pieces, you should have a storage box or bag to keep it in. A large plastic ice cream container works great.

of the plate. Using a straight edge, connect the three marks with a line, Fig. 1, and then cut out the triangle pattern from the paper plate. Now you have a template. Check to make sure that each side of the triangle template is the same length—they should be. Use the template as a guide, and trace the triangle pattern on the face of all the plates. Because some paper plates are very dished, it is sometimes easier to use the template to mark only the edges of the plates with the triangle pattern, connecting the marks with a straight edge and line. Whichever way you find works best, you must press down hard with the

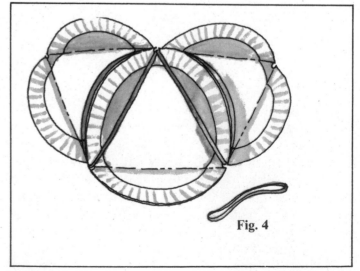

Fig. 4

# Pea and toothpick building

# Pea and toothpick building

This is so nifty. Toothpick rods and pea connectors let you build the most incredible structures and abstract versions of anything—flat patterns, domes, geometric forms, or the Empire State Building.

Construction play increases skills by demanding dexterity, imagination, and creativity. There is no "right way" to do PEA AND TOOTHPICK BUILDING, so there is no wrong way either. Three-year-olds and adult engineers are equally fascinated. It's very inexpensive, and the structures you build are permanent. They stay attached, to be used as ornaments, mobiles, toys, or whatever.

| MATERIALS | TOOLS |
|---|---|
| dried whole peas | large bowl |
| toothpicks | |
| water | |

## CONSTRUCTION

The peas must be prepared ahead of time. Pour a package of dried peas into a large bowl of water, making sure the water completely covers the peas by an inch, Fig. 1. Let the peas soak at least six to nine hours. It's sometimes best to do the pea preparation just before you go to bed, so the peas will soak overnight. That avoids the uncertainty of "are they ready yet." The soaking will soften the peas just enough, but there's little problem of oversoaking. (If the peas stay in the water for more than a couple of days, they will begin to sprout, and that's fun also.) Gather a box or two

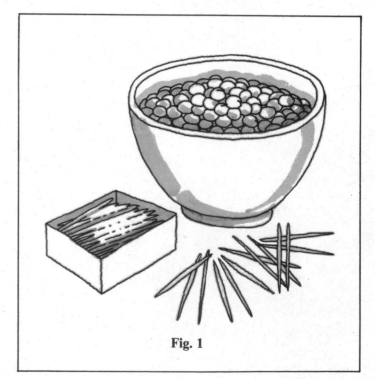

Fig. 1

of toothpicks. The round ones work best, but if all you have are flat toothpicks, that's okay too. Building is done by using the peas as connectors and sticking the toothpicks into them, Fig. 2. The smaller peas hold best. Constructions can be as simple or complex as you want, but you should complete whatever you build at one time, and then put the construction aside to dry. In about a day, the peas will dry out and shrink, making a strong joint. See? Isn't it nifty?

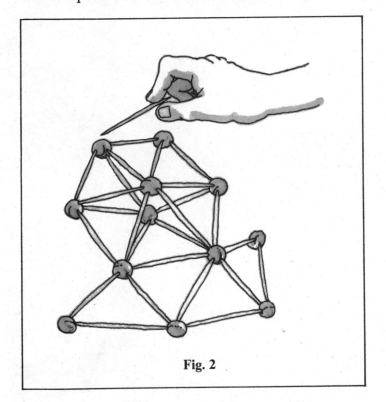

Fig. 2

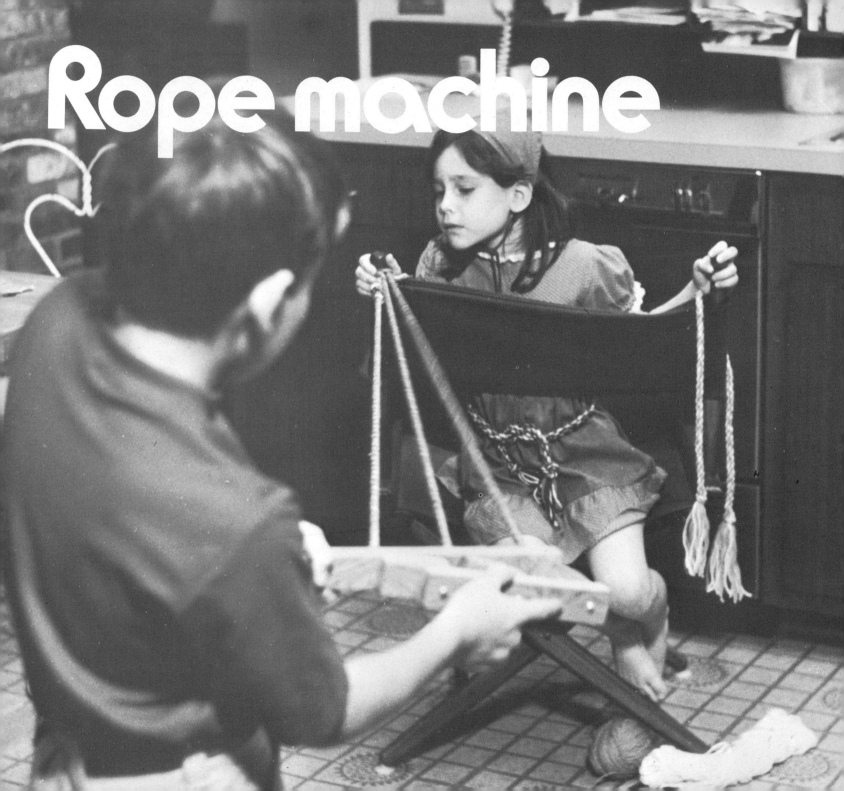

# Rope machine

# Rope machine

Did you ever wonder how rope is made? Maybe it's not one of the great mysteries of life, but fun to know anyway. The ROPE MACHINE is a hand version of the big machines used in rope factories—the process has been the same for thousands of years. The time it takes to construct the rope machine is well worth the fine results it will produce. You are making a tool. Once you have built the machine, any amount and type of rope can be made, and the results come fast. You can make fat or thin ropes, decorative ropes of multicolored yarns, strong work ropes, long or short ropes, or ropes for braiding. You might try belts or jump ropes too.

## MATERIALS

wood stripping
3 wood screws
3 screw hooks

## TOOLS

saw        ruler
drill       sandpaper
pencil      screwdriver

## CONSTRUCTION

As long as the ROPE MACHINE works right mechanically, it doesn't matter how you have

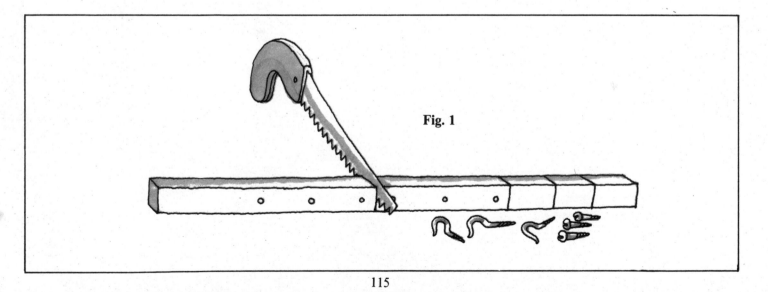

Fig. 1

built it, or what it looks like. So feel free to substitute your own ideas and materials.

Mark off a length of wood stripping into two pieces approximately 13, and 8 inches long, and three pieces, each 2 1/2 inches long. Drill holes where you see the small circles in Fig. 1 (six in all). The drilled holes should be generously larger than the thickness of the wood screws and screw hooks. Cut the wood stripping to size, sand smooth, and assemble the parts as shown in Fig. 2. The wood screws and screw hooks fit loosely through the drilled holes, and fasten securely in the three short center blocks. Don't tighten the screws and hooks all the way. When completed, the ROPE MACHINE should easily rotate all three hooks in unison.

## ROPE MAKING

The instructions for making rope might sound complicated, but the process is quite simple. Refer to the illustrations so that you don't get lost in the words.

Any combination of yarn, string, or thread can be used to make rope. Yarns of different color

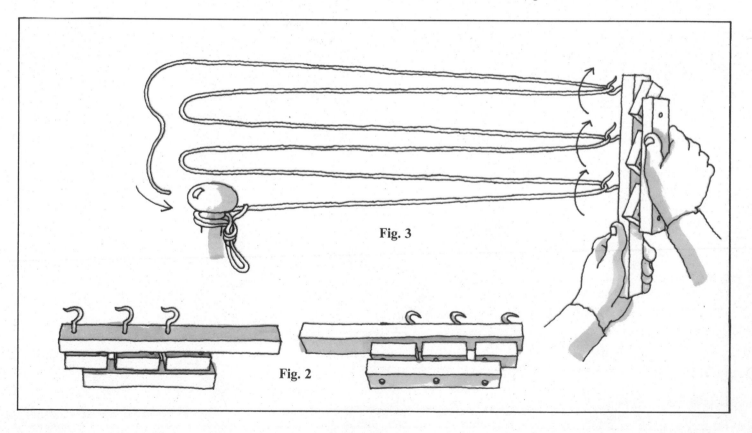

Fig. 3

Fig. 2

and thickness can be strung side by side on the ROPE MACHINE to create fat or thin ropes, or interesting textures and designs. You need to start with yarn about eight times the length of the finished rope you want to make. If you are combining yarns, tie the ends together in a loop that will slip over a door knob. Either way, string up the yarns as shown in Fig. 3: door knob to first hook, to door knob to second hook, to door knob to third hook, to door knob, making a loop to slip over the knob. (You can repeat the stringing a second or third time to make fatter ropes.) It's easier if someone can hold the ROPE MACHINE, or else place it on a chair and run the yarns back of the chair. The ROPE MACHINE should be held about one third further from the door knob than the length of rope you want to make.

Keep the yarn taut, and crank the machine in a clockwise direction. You'll have to move forward while cranking because the twisting takes up some of the yarn's length. Keep cranking until the twists are tight, but don't let the strands kink. The more turns you make, the tighter the finished rope will be. Have someone hold the ROPE MACHINE, or place it over the chair back, Fig. 4.

Carefully remove the yarn from the door knob, and with your other hand grab the three strands of twisted yarn. Keep the strands taut while pulling the end and twisting the three parts together in a counterclockwise direction. Continue until the full length of rope is made. Hold the rope tightly while removing the yarn from the hooks. Tie both ends of the rope in a single knot to prevent unraveling. You can snip off the loop ends to make a tassel.

The rope is complete.

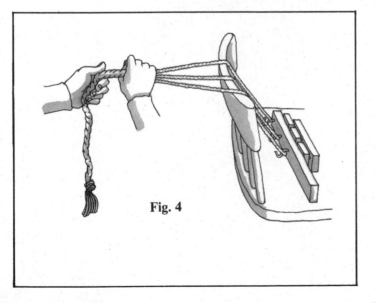

Fig. 4

# Picture puzzles

# Picture puzzles

While growing up, jigsaw puzzles can be a way of life.

The four- and five-year-old can usually handle large, simple puzzles of ten to fifteen pieces, as long as the pieces are fairly thick so they fit together easily. But the older kid—six to seven and up—is able to attack more complex puzzles in a more sophisticated way. The pieces don't have to be big and fat, and there can be many more parts—twenty-five or maybe a hundred. Older kids are more systematic, and look for clues in the pieces and in the picture pattern. The straight-edge and corner pieces are always sorted out first . . .

PICTURE PUZZLES are a way to turn any paper picture into a "plastic" jigsaw puzzle. You might try making puzzles from road maps, postcards, posters, magazine covers, or some of the beautifully illustrated advertising circulars that come with junk mail. Because the puzzle pieces will be thin, PICTURE PUZZLES are best suited for the six-year-old-and-up age group—although a four-year-old would enjoy making the puzzle by cutting out the pieces (as long as you don't mind a few picture details being snipped off).

After the puzzle has been made, have a container to put the pieces in. A large manila envelope with a clasp is good. Some people are annoyed when they find a piece missing.

| MATERIALS | TOOLS |
|---|---|
| paper picture | mixing bowl |
| white glue | mixing spoon |
| wax paper | scissors |
| water | |

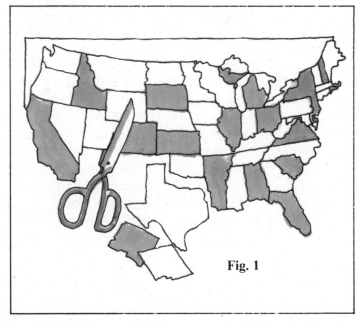

**Fig. 1**

119

## CONSTRUCTION

Pick your own puzzle picture. Although any paper picture of any size will work fine, maps of the United States are a big favorite—and you can get them free from oil companies or automobile clubs. With a scissors, cut the picture into any number of puzzle pieces, but don't get too small. The pieces don't have to be in the traditional puzzle shapes—make up your own shapes. If you're using a U.S. map, cut out each state, Fig. 1.

Make a mixture of white glue and water, using about four times as much glue as water. All together about a cup (8 ounces) will do. Stir the mixture in a large bowl for a minute, until it is nice and syrupy. Alongside the bowl put a few sheets of wax paper—they must be flat and smooth. Now dip each of the puzzle parts in the glue mixture, Fig. 2. Make sure the pieces are completely covered, but be careful because the paper is wet and could easily tear. Dip one puzzle piece at a time. Let the excess glue drip off, and lay the piece down flat on the wax paper—picture side up, Fig. 3. After the pieces have had a chance to dry a bit—usually about an hour—lay another piece of wax paper over the puzzle parts and weight them down with a few books. The weight will keep the puzzle pieces flat while the glue dries hard overnight. The glue looks white while it's wet, but will dry completely clear. After they dry, the paper puzzle pieces will have a smooth, shiny, plasticlike coating that's flexible and strong enough to resist tearing—and last through many, many playings.

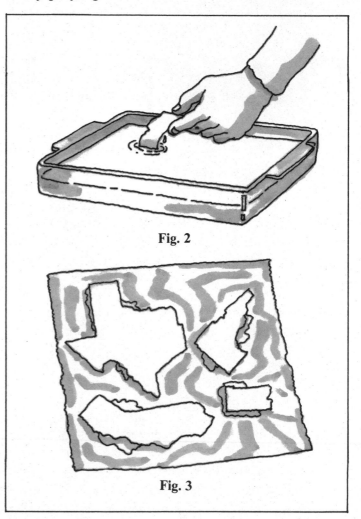

Fig. 2

Fig. 3

# Clip hangers

# Clip hangers

Start by tying one CLIP HANGER to a dangling piece of string. Then hang two CLIP HANGERS from the first, and down you go. This is one of the only building toys that starts at the top and builds downwards. There are many possible ways to connect the pieces, and you can expand your construction up, down, and across. But watch your balance. If the CLIP HANGERS get too lopsided, they can be in for a big fall. CLIP HANGERS may be taken apart to use over and over again, or the finished mobile may be hung in a sunny window to reflect the light from the metal parts. This toy can give purpose to the compulsive paper clip bender.

## MATERIALS

paper clips
string

## CONSTRUCTION

Look at the illustrations and you will see how to do it. Move the loop up to build wide. Move the loop down to build narrow.

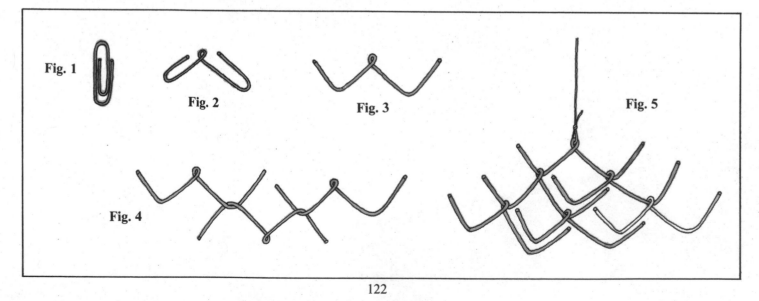

Fig. 1

Fig. 2

Fig. 3

Fig. 4

Fig. 5

# ACTION TOYS

City Kite

# City Kite

With most kites, you need lots of open space—a place away from tall buildings, trees, and wires. The CITY KITE will fly just great in a big open space, but it will fly just as well in a vacant lot, from the sidewalk, at the playground, or out a window. The CITY KITE is small and light. It goes about 10 to 50 feet high, and does its best to stay out of trouble.

| MATERIALS | TOOLS |
| --- | --- |
| 6 drinking straws | scissors |
|   (paper or plastic) | pencil |
| light string | |
| tissue paper | |
| glue or tape | |

## CONSTRUCTION

Make the kite frame by threading a length of light string through the straws. A good way to get the string through is to suck it through—start the string in one end of the straw, and suck on the other end. Carefully follow the illustrations. First tie three straws together in a triangle, Fig. 1, add two more to make another triangle, Fig. 2, and then add the last one, Fig. 3, to form a tetrahedron—a form that's something like a pyramid. When tying the straws together, pull the string

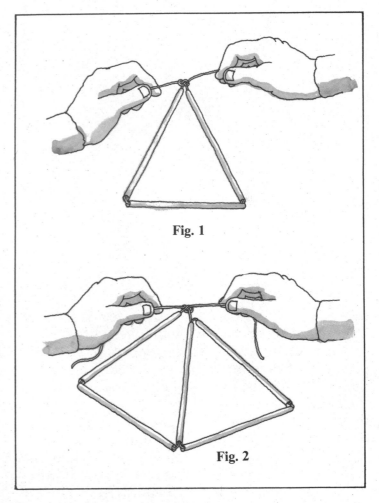

Fig. 1

Fig. 2

125

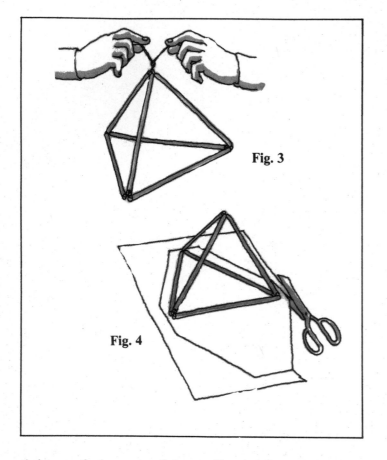

Fig. 3

Fig. 4

won't fly well, if at all. Carefully copy the rigging shown in Fig. 5. The top string of the bridle is attached about one third down from the top front edge of the kite, and it's tied through the paper, around the straw. The lower bridle string is attached to the very bottom of the front edge, and it's a little bit longer than the top string. Attach a roll of light kite string at the point where the two bridle strings meet. Make a good knot. Cut some 2-inch-wide strips of tissue paper, and tie them together to make a tail about 3 feet long. Attach the tail to the bottom front edge of the kite.

Successful kite flying depends a lot on experimenting and making small adjustments. Hot days, cool days, windy days, and calm days all affect how well the kite will fly. You might try adding more tail, or changing the lengths of the bridle strings. Hold up the kite and let it catch the wind. Light winds? Try running. If you want to make a kite that flies much higher, try connecting two, three, or more CITY KITES together, using straws and strings as connectors. You can stack the kites, or attach them sideways, or both, but the front edges must all face the same direction. You'll have to do your own experimenting to get the bridle just right.

tight, and tie a good knot. Two sides of the kite frame need to be covered with a very light paper or thin plastic wrap. Tissue paper or cleaner's plastic clothes wrap works very well. Remember that the lighter the kite, the better it will fly. Using the kite frame as a guide, cut the paper about an inch bigger on the sides, as shown in Fig. 4. Glue or tape the edges over the kite frame—a little bit of glue works much better than a lot. Making the bridle (the string harness that attaches to the kite) in just the right way is very important, or the kite

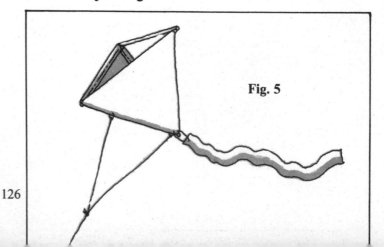

Fig. 5

Pocket parachute

# Pocket parachute

Almost every kid tries to make a parachute at some time, usually to give a small personal belonging a launch up into the sky (and then, hopefully, a slow ride back to earth). Parachutes can also be made to travel great distances on windy days, to play catch games, or merely to float in the sky. The POCKET PARACHUTE has been designed with just the right combination of materials for floating slowly to the ground—especially on days with a gentle breeze.

| MATERIALS | TOOLS |
|---|---|
| plastic bag | ruler |
| string | scissors |
| Tinker Toy connector | |

## CONSTRUCTION

Find a plastic bag or something similar, like cleaner's plastic wrap. Plastic works better than paper or cloth because it is very light and strong. The more brightly colored the plastic, the better the parachute can be seen—like the colorful parachutes that float a space capsule down to earth. Measure and then cut a piece of the plastic 12 inches square. Punch a hole in each corner, but not too close to the edges or the hole might tear out. The hole can be made with a pencil point or

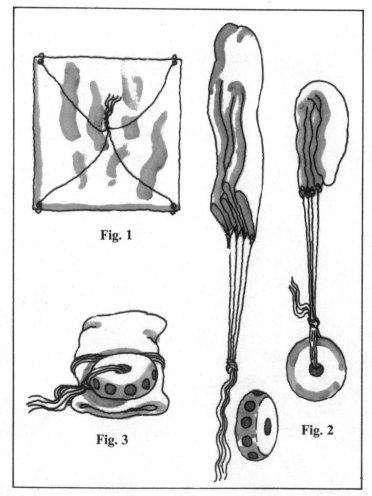

Fig. 1

Fig. 2

Fig. 3

128

a nail. Cut four pieces of light string, each about 12 inches long. Tie a string to each corner of the plastic by putting the string through the hole and tying a knot. Lay the plastic flat, and bring all the strings in towards the center. Tie all four strings in a knot where they meet, Fig. 1, and then tie the Tinker Toy connector at the end of the strings, Fig. 2. If you don't have a Tinker Toy connector, you might try using fifteen paper clips—they both weigh about the same. Fold up the parachute as shown in Fig. 3, and now you're ready for launching. You can throw the parachute up in the air, or experiment with a catapult launcher. A simple catapult can be made from a wood stick about 2 feet long and a fist size rock. Put the rock on the ground, and then put the stick on the rock about one third in from the end of the stick. Place the folded parachute on the very end of the long side of the stick. Now stomp your foot on the short end of the stick, hard and fast, Fig. 4. The parachute will shoot up into the air. Be very careful to keep yourself and others out of the way of the parachute as it's being launched. Now it's up to you to try your own ideas by making modifications on the POCKET PARACHUTE, or designing your own. Make the strings a little longer, use a round piece of plastic, or snip a hole about the size of a penny in the center of the parachute. What do you think will happen?

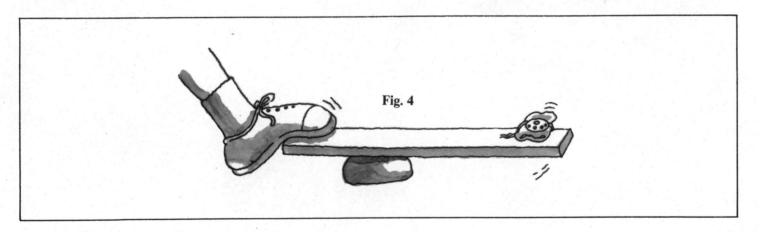

Fig. 4

# Tire ring swing

# Tire ring swing

With almost hypnotic power, a swing can keep you occupied for hours. Regular old tire swings have been around for a long time, but this TIRE RING SWING is different. You can climb snugly into it, or turn it upside down to make a pair of acrobat rings. Maybe you can go on to invent a whole circus. The TIRE RING SWING is also safer than most because the pocket seat holds you firmly, and you can wrap your hands securely through the rings. If someone should accidentally get bumped, the rubber swing doesn't give such a hard knock.

Before making the swing, be sure you have a good place to hang it from—a strong tree limb, porch beam, doorway, or a regular swing frame.

## MATERIALS

old auto tire
strong rope

## TOOLS

electric saber saw
chalk

## CONSTRUCTION

Find an old auto tire. Any size will do, but it might be fun to use a small tire for a little kid's swing, and a big tire for a big kid's. With a piece of chalk or soap, draw the cutout pattern on the tire, as shown in Fig. 1. There are no exact dimensions, but be sure the seat part seems about the right size for sitting. Follow the chalk line, and cut away part of the tire. Tires are made with very strong cords molded inside the rubber, so they are

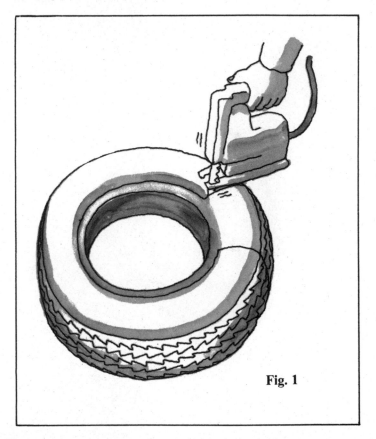

**Fig. 1**

very difficult to cut. An electric saber saw with a fine tooth blade will do the job quickly, but you must be very careful and watch what you're doing. If you want to try a handsaw, be sure you have plenty of muscle—and time.

Now the swing part is finished and only needs to be hung up. Use a piece of 1/2-inch manila rope (available at most hardware or boat stores), or something equally as strong. Don't try to use clothes line—it's much too weak. Tie a length of rope to each of the rings, Fig. 2. Tie a good double knot. Find a place to hang the swing about 7 or 8 feet off the ground. The swing seat should be low enough for your feet to touch the ground. For safety, there should be a lot of free space around the swing.

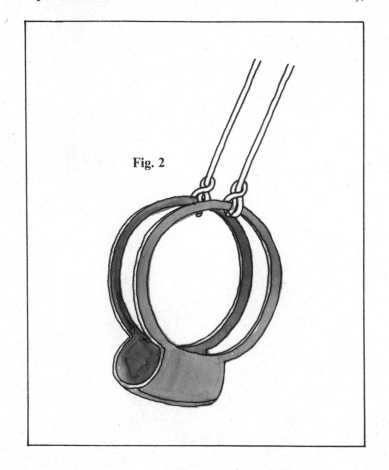

Fig. 2

Bull roarer

# Bull roarer

The way Indian folklore tells it, the BULL ROARER was once used to imitate the sound of onrushing winds in the hope of bringing on rain. The wood of the BULL ROARER often came from a tree that had been struck by lightning, and the roarer was aptly decorated with drawings of lightning and thunderbird symbols. The "moaning stick," as it was sometimes called, also did a pretty good job of scaring off demons and evil spirits. And with all that magic noisemaking, the BULL ROARER is just a thin piece of wood you fling around on the end of a string. Even though the roarer is quite simple to make, there are many different shapes and sizes you might try—and no two will sound exactly alike.

## MATERIALS

thin scrap of wood
string

## TOOLS

sandpaper
drill

## CONSTRUCTION

There are no exact dimensions for making a BULL ROARER; just use a small, thin, flat scrap of wood. The thinner and lighter the wood, the safer everyone will feel about something that's going to be swinging around in the air. The shape does not have to be rectangular. You might try rounding one end or giving a symmetrical shape to the sides. The side edges should be slightly tapered, though, using sandpaper (or file, or penknife).

In one end of the wood, centered near the edge, drill a small hole for attaching a string; see illustration. The hole can also be made with a nail and hammer. Tie on a length of string—about 3 or 4 feet. Except for any color or decoration you might be inclined to apply, the BULL ROARER is ready for testing. Tightly hold the free end of the string, and quickly spin the roarer in circles over your head—or in front of you. The faster you spin, the higher pitched the sound. If you don't hear the "roar" right away, keep on spinning, or stop and start again. The sound will come and go, but that's part of the magic.

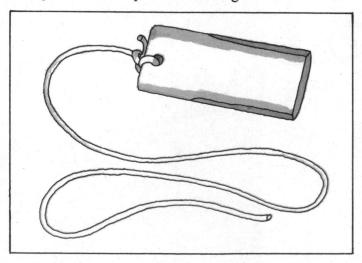

# Soap bubbler

# Soap bubbler

Almost no one outgrows the fun of blowing soap bubbles. There's something marvelous about those beautiful floating spheres with strange rainbowlike patterns, and few can resist the temptation to join someone who's blowing bubbles. Pretty soon you're having a soap bubble contest to see who can blow the biggest bubble, the longest lasting, or the highest floating.

There is actually much more to the soap bubble than you might imagine. For example, if you think soap bubbles must burst after a few seconds, think again. Scientists have been able to keep a soap bubble whole for more than two years. Also, a soap bubble is one of the thinnest things that can be seen without a microscope. In fact, a soap bubble is five thousand times thinner than a hair from your head. That's pretty hard to imagine.

## MAKING SOAPY WATER

Fill the bottom of something like a shallow sauce or cake pan with about 1/2 inch of clean water. Add three or four big squirts of a liquid dishwashing detergent (you might also try other types of soaps). Mix the solution gently so you *don't* make a lot of suds. To do a super bubble solution that will let you blow bigger and longer

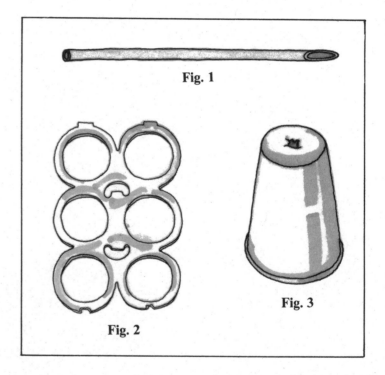

Fig. 1

Fig. 2

Fig. 3

lasting bubbles, add a small amount of glycerin. Glycerin is safe, and can be bought at most any drugstore.

## MAKING BUBBLERS

Drinking Straw

Slice the end off a drinking straw, Fig. 1. The sliced end is dipped in the soapy solution, and you blow (gently) through the plain end.

## Six-Pack Holder

A plastic soda or beer can six-pack holder is great for making lots of bubbles at a time, Fig. 2. Dip the thing into the soapy water and wave it through the air.

## Drinking Cup

Poke a small hole in the bottom of a disposable drinking cup, Fig. 3. Dip the big opening of the cup into the soapy stuff and gently blow through the little hole.

## Plastic Funnel

Blow through the small end of a plastic funnel, or cut the funnel in two parts to make a big ring and a small blowing tube, Fig. 4.

## Your Hands

Just your hands dipped in the bubble solution can make some incredibly large soap bubbles. Hold your hands together to make a cup, but with a small opening at the bottom, Fig. 5. Hold your cupped hands about a foot in front of your mouth and blow.

You can blow bubbles through a pipe or the ring part of a mason jar top, Fig. 6. When you blow bubbles through a pipe or straw, the warm air from your lungs will cause the bubbles to float up because it is lighter than the air outside. You might think that soap bubbles are very fragile, and burst as soon as they touch some object. Try bouncing a soap bubble around on a piece of woolen cloth—you'll be surprised at what happens.

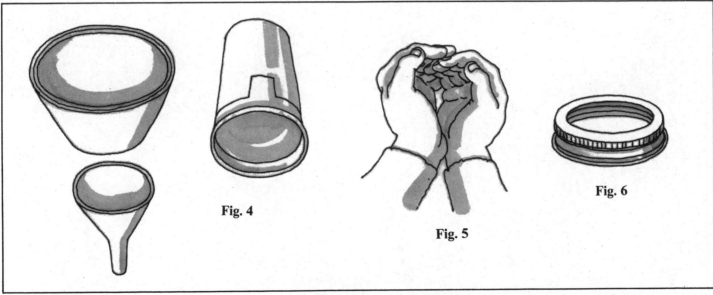

Fig. 4

Fig. 5

Fig. 6

# Wing and helicopter

# Wing and helicopter

Whether from inventiveness or just plain boredom, most everyone tries as a kid to fold the "perfect" paper plane—a plane that gently soars like a sea gull the full length of the room. Up until now, the favorite paper plane has been the "dart," which is relatively easy to make, but erratic in its reliability. Well, teachers beware! The search for the better paper plane ends here. The PAPER WING is a breakthrough in ultimate simplicity, with an unblemished flight record (to date). And for those with limited flying space (or a lesser paper budget) there is the equally flightworthy Z HELICOPTER.

MATERIALS

paper

CONSTRUCTION

PAPER WING

Fig. 1) Cut a regular notebook size sheet of paper in half. Each half will make a plane, so put one aside for now.

Fig. 2) Fold the paper in half and crease it—then open it up again.

Fig. 3) Fold one of the flaps over to the center line and crease.

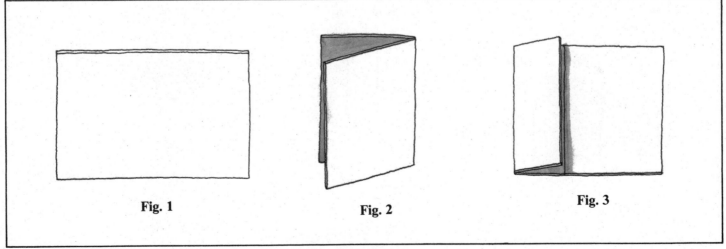

Fig. 1          Fig. 2          Fig. 3

Fig. 4) Fold the folded flap over again to the center line and crease.

Fig. 5) Now fold the entire folded flap over again *on* the center line.

Fig. 6) Give the PAPER WING some curve by drawing it over the sharp edge of a table. The folded section should be on the inside.

Hold the PAPER WING in your fingertips—folded part forward and facing up. Hold your hand up high and release the plane with a gentle push.

## Z HELICOPTER

1) Cut a strip of notebook size paper across the short length, Fig. 1.
2) Fold the strip in thirds and crease.
3) Open up the strip until it holds the approximate shape illustrated in Fig. 2.

Hold the Z HELICOPTER in the center with your fingertips. Reach up high, or stand on a stool, or go to the top of a flight of stairs. With a slight flipping motion of the wrist, release the Z.

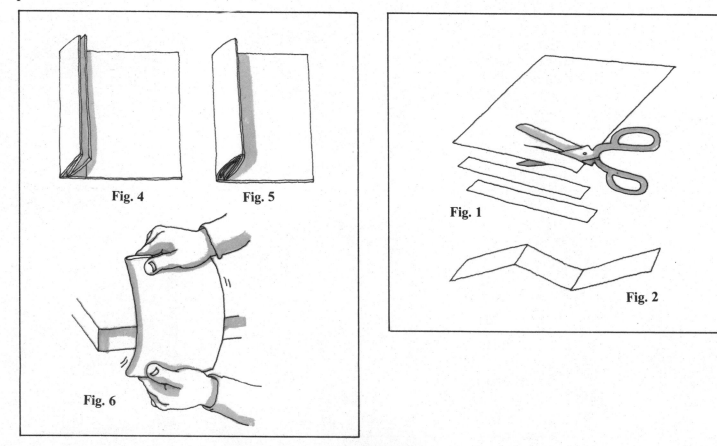

Fig. 4  Fig. 5

Fig. 6

Fig. 1

Fig. 2

**Dancing man**

# Dancing man

Like so many other American folk toys, the DANCING MAN was a "demonstration" toy—a toy intended to amuse the child but not necessarily one he played with. Just as there is music to listen to and music to play, there are some toys to play with and some toys to watch.

The DANCING MAN is a wood doll with jointed arms and legs that can do an amazingly realistic tap dance to any music you sing or play. In some ways it's an actual rhythm instrument. Working it takes practice, though; you'll need patience and the guidance of a grown-up. Maybe it would be fair if this toy belonged to the grown-ups. They could play it for you on request and perhaps give you a turn.

## MATERIALS

1/4-inch-thick wood scrap
1-inch-thick wood scrap
wood dowel
wood screws
drawer knob or thread spool
tracing or writing paper

## TOOLS

coping saw
drill
screwdriver
sandpaper
glue
pencil

## CONSTRUCTION

Making the DANCING MAN does require

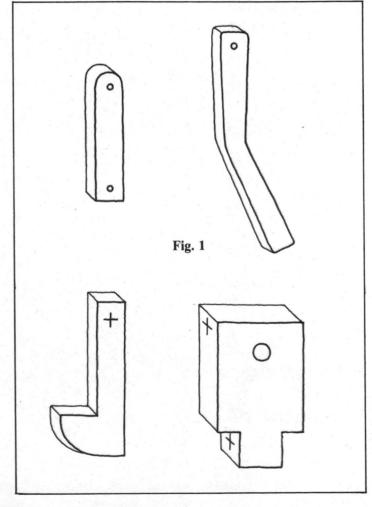

Fig. 1

some careful cutting and fitting of the parts. So unless you're handy yourself, have someone who is good at making things help you out. From Fig. 1, trace the body parts. Trace the arm and leg parts twice. The shape of the parts does not have to be exact. You might want to add your own little touches of design.

With just a little bit of glue, stick the tracings of the arm and leg parts on a piece of 1/4-inch-thick wood (or hardboard), and cut out the shapes with a coping saw. Stick the tracing of the body on a 1-inch scrap of wood, and then cut out the shape. Drill holes (a little larger than the screws you're going to use) in the arms and legs at those places marked with a circle on the pattern. Sand smooth the sides and edges of all the parts. Sand off the tracing paper. Drill a hole about halfway through the center of the body part. The hole should be just big enough to fit the long wood dowel tightly. Find a big drawer knob or empty thread spool to use for a head.

Assemble all the parts together, using small and short wood screws through the drilled holes and into the places marked with a cross on the illustrations, Fig. 2. Don't tighten the screws all the way—the arms and legs should swing quite freely. The long dowel stick should be glued in place.

The dancing paddle is made from another piece of 1/4-inch wood about 5 inches wide and 20 or more inches long, Fig. 3. You might want to decorate the doll—that's optional.

## DANCING

Play a record or sing a song—something with a fast rhythm. Sit on one end of the wood paddle, on a hard surface like a bench, table edge, metal or wooden chair. Keep time to the music by hitting the end of the paddle with your hand or thumb. Hold the DANCING MAN by the dowel so he is just above the paddle. Watch him dance. The vibration of the paddle hitting the doll's feet is what does it. You can invent some dancing "tricks" by holding the doll in various positions above the paddle—sitting, on his knees, or tilted to one side.

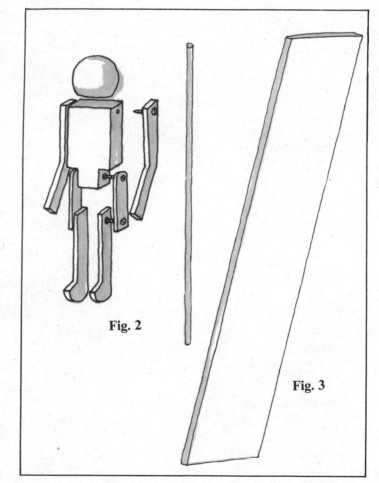

Fig. 2

Fig. 3

# Propeller stick

# Propeller stick

American Indians know the magic of how to make the propeller spin, stop, and then spin in the other direction. If you know the magic, you can pretend to make the PROPELLER STICK work as a lie detector. Get the propeller spinning and ask a question. If the answer is yes, the propeller will continue to spin in the same direction. If the answer is no, the propeller will stop and then start spinning the other way. Actually, there is no magic to it at all—if you know the trick.

## MATERIALS

small sticks
headed nail

## TOOLS

penknife
hammer

## CONSTRUCTION

Cut a stick, or a piece of a dead tree branch, about 8 to 12 inches long, and whittle half the length of it down to bare wood. (Always be careful when using a knife. Never point the sharp edge or tip of the blade towards yourself or anyone close by, and carve with the knife blade cutting in the direction away from you.) On the whittled end of the stick, cut about six or eight notches in a row, Fig. 1. Make the propeller from a smaller stick about 3 inches long, and whittle it down to bare wood—it does not need to be the

shape of a propeller at all. Measure to the center of the propeller, and make a hole through it slightly bigger than the thickness of the headed nail. You can make the hole with a drill, or by hammering a fatter nail through, wiggling it around, and then pulling it out. Mount the pro-

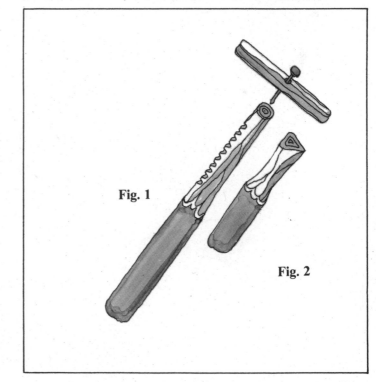

Fig. 1

Fig. 2

peller onto the notched end of the bigger stick with the headed nail, Fig. 1, but don't drive the nail in all the way. Leave it out just a little so that the propeller spins very easily. If necessary, balance the propeller by carving chips off the heavier end.

The rubbing stick is made from another wood piece about as round as the notched stick, but only half as long, Fig. 2. Whittle down one end of the rubbing stick to a slightly pointed edge that will be used for rubbing the notches. Now you're ready to try the "trick." Hold the propeller stick in one hand, and point it slightly down. Hold the rubbing stick in the other hand, and rub the pointed edge back and forth over the notches. Try rubbing fast then slow, easy then hard, until you find just the right rhythm and pressure to make the propeller spin. If you have trouble, try holding the propeller stick a little closer to the notches or a little further away from the notches. To make the propeller change direction, put your pointing finger out along the side of the notched stick, Fig. 3. Which way does the propeller spin? Now take your pointing finger back, and put your thumb out along the other side of the stick, Fig. 4. Does the propeller change direction? It should. The hand is quicker than the lie.

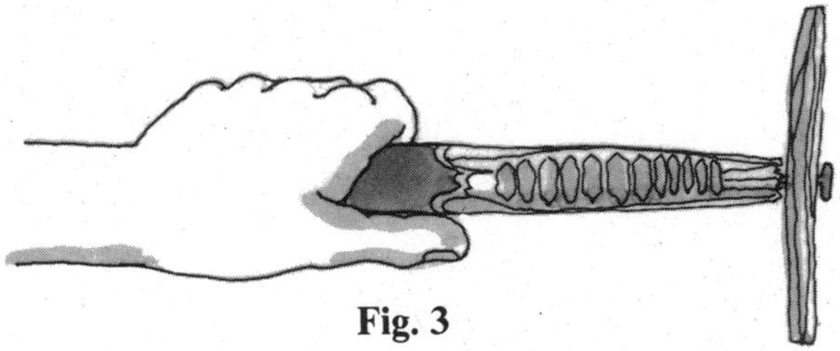

Fig. 3

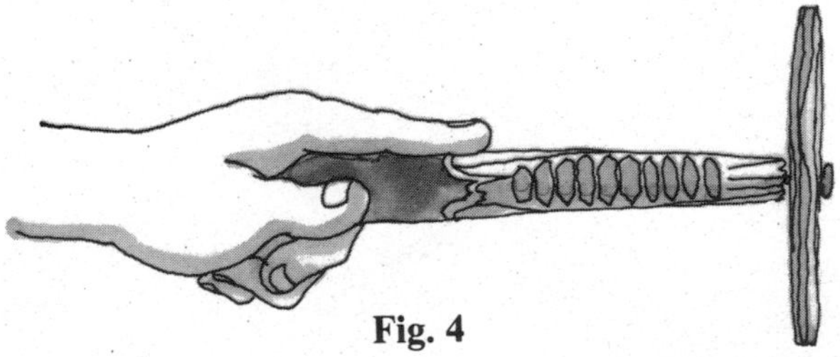

Fig. 4

milk carton boat

# milk carton boat

A kid's sailboat is one of the oldest of the traditional toys. It can be anything from a three-masted schooner model to a wooden shingle with a handkerchief sail. Without much difficulty, a kid and a boat somehow always find a pond, puddle, or park fountain. And two kids with boats will always devise races or imaginative ways of transporting goods from one shore across to the other.

The MILK CARTON SAILBOAT design is clearly as simple and elegant as it is seaworthy. The two halves of the milk carton act as large pontoons to keep the boat upright and sailing straight—they also make good compartments for carrying cargo. Milk cartons are made of plastic-coated paper which is waterproof, but most paper plates are not. If you accidentally get the sail soaking wet, you had better have a spare handy. Unless you intend to sail in a puddle or small pond, it's a good idea to tie a length of sewing thread to the end of the boat so you can pull it back.

## MATERIALS

milk carton
paper plate

## TOOLS

penknife

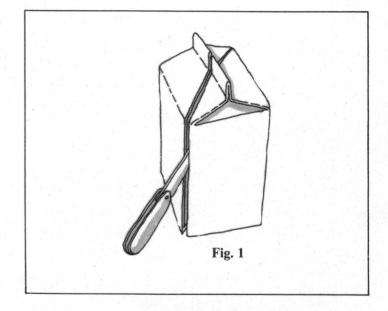

Fig. 1

## CONSTRUCTION

Save a paper milk carton—either the quart or half-gallon size will do. Rinse it out thoroughly. Using a penknife, cut down one long edge of the milk carton, and diagonally across the top and bottom, Fig. 1. Hinge open the carton, Fig. 2. Continue to fold the carton back on itself and make a knife cut about one third of the way back from the front of the boat to accommodate the paper plate sail, Fig. 2. The slot should go half-way down through the two thicknesses of the carton, and be angled slightly to match the angle of the paper plate edge.

Fold open the two boat halves and fit the paper plate into the slot to form the sail. Many boats have sails with colorful decorations. That's easy enough. Just crayon, paint, or use color markers to create a sail design. Now take to the water and wind.

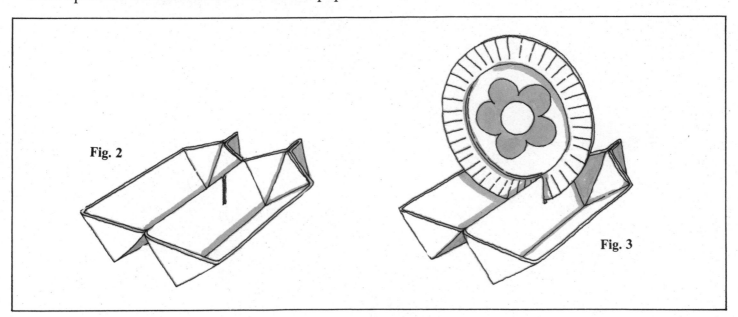

Fig. 2

Fig. 3

# DESIGN TOYS

# Color jars

# Color jars

Half the fun is making these color jars, the other half is discovering what you can do with them. You can make all the colors of the rainbow by using only red, blue, yellow, and green food coloring—and you'll also probably make some nonrainbow colors that no one has ever invented. Not only can you experiment with mixing colors, but you can decide what to call them—things like "raspberry pink," "gorgeous green," or "yucky yellow." The COLOR JARS can be stacked on a sunny windowsill to let beautiful patterns of colored light stream into a room. If you look through the jars, you can change the color of the world. What do you think happens when each eye looks through a different COLOR JAR, or when you look through two or three COLOR JARS in a row?

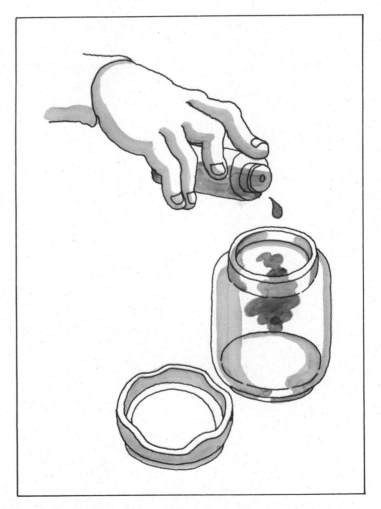

## MATERIALS

small baby food jars
  with lids
food coloring
water

## TOOLS

small spoon
paper towels

## MIXING

Making a little bit of a mess is part of playing, but try to do your color mixing outside, or in the sink, and keep a few paper towels handy for wiping up. Collect a bunch of small baby food jars that have screw-on lids. Baby food jars are made of very thick glass, and there is little chance of breakage. Still, you should always be careful. Wash out the jars and scrape off the labels. Sometimes the labels are easier to get off if you soak the jars in warm water for a few minutes. After the jars have been cleaned, fill each one with water almost to the very top. Now you're ready to start color mixing. Add 1 or 2 drops of food coloring to a jar, and stir with a small spoon, Fig. 1. If you want to make the color a little darker, add another drop or two of the food color. When you think that the color is exactly right, screw on the jar lid very tightly. Make some more COLOR JARS, using the other food colors and mixing drops of different colors together. You should experiment and invent your own color recipes, but here are a few to get you started.

to make

| | | | | | | |
|---|---|---|---|---|---|---|
| ORANGE | mix | 1 drop | RED | with | 2 drops | YELLOW |
| LIME | | 3 | YELLOW | | 1 | GREEN |
| PURPLE | | 2 | RED | | 1 | BLUE |

# Cardboard weaving

# Cardboard weaving

A kid wants to invent something unique and altogether his own. When you can take some cardboard, string, yarn, and other household scraps and create your own personal weave, you feel proud and confident. Cardboard weaving looms offer a wide range of possibilities. You can make weavings in different shapes and work them in different materials. Try making interesting patterns and projects like waistbands, purses, potholders, blankets, rugs, or wall hangings.

## MATERIALS

cardboard
pocket comb
yarn, string, or other
    material suitable
    for weaving

## TOOLS

scissors
paper hole punch
ruler
pencil

## CONSTRUCTION

Find a piece of stiff scrap cardboard—from a shirt, gift box or shoe box. Draw the shape of the piece you want to weave and cut it out on the cardboard. Although you can weave almost any shape cardboard loom, it is probably easiest to start with a simple square or rectangle. With a ruler and pencil, mark off 1/4-inch spaces along two opposite sides of the cardboard, Fig. 1. With

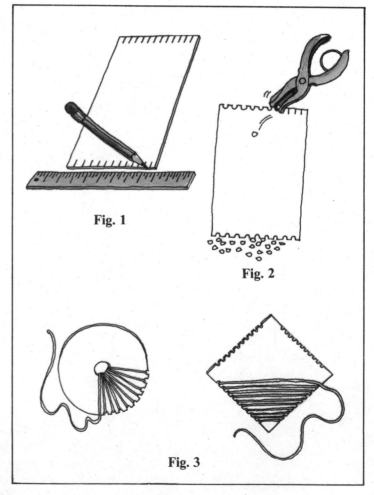

Fig. 1

Fig. 2

Fig. 3

a paper hole punch make a notch—about half a circle or a little more—at each pencil mark, Fig. 2. The notches can also be cut with a scissors. The loom is now ready to be strung with the "warp" threads. The warp can be made from a long piece of yarn, thread, fishing line, or any type of string. Start the warp at one edge of the cardboard, and wind it around and around in the notches, going completely across the cardboard, Fig. 3. To start and end the warp (so it doesn't unwind), you can use two small pieces of tape, or cut a small slit in each side of the cardboard loom, and push the beginning and end of the warp thread into the slits. With another piece of scrap cardboard make a "shuttle" to hold the weaving yarn. The shuttle should be cut out with big notches in both ends, as in Fig. 4. Pick a piece of yarn or string to weave, and wind a length of it around the shuttle. Begin weaving by pushing the shuttle over and under the warp threads all the way across the loom, then go back in the other direction, this time going over and under the warp threads in the opposite order. Each time you bring the shuttle through, pull the yarn taut to take up slack—but not too tight—and unwind some yarn from the shuttle. After you weave a line, use a pocket comb with big teeth to push the woven lines snuggly together, Fig. 4. While weaving, you can change colors and textures by changing yarns on the shuttle. Just tie the new yarn onto the end of the previous piece. You don't necessarily have to weave with yarn on a shuttle, or with yarn at all. Try weaving with tissue paper, scraps of cloth, paper strips, long grass, or whatever you think of trying, and on both sides of the loom.

When the weaving is finished, you can either leave it on the loom—to be used, perhaps, as a wall decoration—or you can take it off by cutting the warp threads on the back of the loom and tying them together in pairs at the ends of the woven piece. Weaving is a skill and an art, so it might take some practice and patience to get things to come out just right, but never be afraid to experiment with your own ideas.

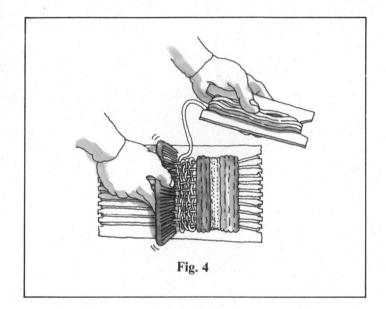

Fig. 4

# Roller and stamp printing

# Roller and stamp printing

With a little experimentation and curiosity, you can print with almost any object on almost any material—like the kids doing ROLLER AND STAMP PRINTING in the photograph. Sometimes the printing techniques are quite strange, as well as the resulting image. Most grown-ups think first about kids printing something "useful" like Christmas cards, invitations, or something to decorate the walls. That's okay, but kids would rather mess around with printing, find out what the materials can do, and then take on a project. Try mapping out a city or village on a large piece of paper, and then filling in the areas with toy objects—sort of like setting up an electric train layout. A roller printer can make continuous roads, rivers, or train tracks, and where the roads cross, or rivers meet tracks, you can stamp a bridge or a road sign. You might roll sidewalks and fences, stamp trees, houses, cars, and people. To do an entire village—many kids join in—you'll need a large piece of paper to print on, like a big newsprint pad, roll of shelf paper or wallpaper (use the back of the wallpaper), newspaper classified section, or even an old cloth sheet.

If there are other kids involved, you might want to talk about planning the design. Each person might have an area of the paper to develop, or a specific job to do—river maker, road maker,

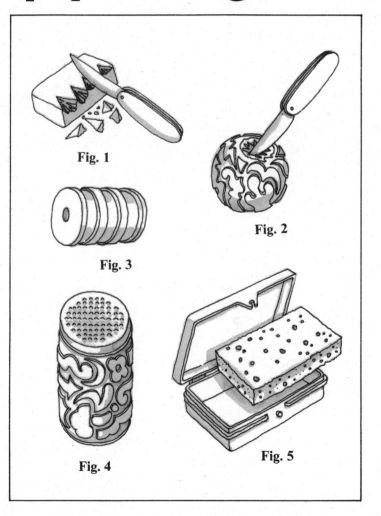

Fig. 1

Fig. 2

Fig. 3

Fig. 4

Fig. 5

bridge maker, and so forth. Even while you're printing, talk about where you might place certain things—the school, post office, food market, bank, and your house. Wouldn't it be fun to have the school next to the circus, and maybe your house between a candy store and the movies? You decide. Don't be too concerned with the scale of things, and don't copy someone else's design or pattern. Once you've mapped out the village with rollers and stamps, add some small toys to give it some form and action. Put cars and trucks on the roads and boats in the rivers; build skyscrapers with blocks, make a mountain from a rock, and let your fingers do the (people) walking.

Being neat with the materials is not nearly so important as confining the mess to one area. Put things away for yourself, clean up after playing. Because you're likely to make lots of different printers, it's a good idea to have a place to store all that stuff—like a plastic ice cream container.

## MATERIALS

almost anything that
   will make an
   interesting outline
   (see below)
white glue
poster paint
soap dish
sponge
paper towels (for cleaning up)

## TOOLS

scissors
penknife
pencil and ball-point
   pen
mixing spoon

## MAKING PRINTERS

Printing stamps can be made from most any hunk of material that can be easily cut—pencil erasers, Fig. 1, rubber balls, Fig. 2, potatoes. Draw a design on the surface and cut away the parts you don't want to print. Remember that the stamps will print backwards. Try it. Stamps can also be made from glueing pieces of material—cloth, tire tube, sponge—onto a wood block. Making a roller printer is just as easy. Put some rubber bands around an empty thread spool, Fig. 3. A tire tube repair kit—the kind that comes in a round box—will make a great roller printer. Cut up the tube patches and stick them on the outside of the round container, Fig. 4. The patch already has sticky stuff on it (peel off the protective backing).

Regular ink pads can be used if you're very careful. The ink, though nontoxic, can make you very sick if you "eat" too much—and that means putting inky fingers in your mouth. And besides, the ink is pretty hard to get off you and your clothes. So to make your own ink stamp pad—safe and washable—cut a piece of sponge to fit the inside of a plastic soap dish, Fig. 5. Mix two parts poster paint with one part white glue, and pour the mixture all over the sponge. A little bit will do—you can always mix up some more. The glue makes the paint stick much better to the printers and the paper. If the stamp pad starts to dry out, add a little water.

Ink the printers by pressing them on the sponge; ink the rollers by moving them back and forth. Now start printing.

Soap crayons

# Soap crayons

Don't worry about making a mess. SOAP CRAYONS are made from pure soap and food coloring, so whatever you draw with them will wipe off bathtubs, sinks, floors, windows—and hands and faces. SOAP CRAYONS add a little soak-time play to the bath routine, and they are great for making disguises on your body. Try a big moustache, a clown face, or make yourself into a monster.

| MATERIALS | TOOLS |
|---|---|
| Ivory Flakes | measuring cup |
| food coloring | spoon |
| water | ice cube tray |

## RECIPE

Pour water into a cup size measuring cup until it reaches the 1/8 mark (1/8 is halfway between the bottom and the 1/4 mark). Fill the rest of the measuring cup to the top with Ivory Flakes. With a spoon, mix the water and soap flakes together. It may seem as if there isn't enough water, but keep mixing and blending until you have a thick soapy paste without any big lumps. Add about 30 or 40 drops of food coloring to the soap mixture, and stir very well until all the white is gone and the soap has color. With the same spoon, scoop out some of the mixture and put it in one of the cube spaces of an ice cube tray. A one-piece plastic ice cube tray works best. Press the soap paste down into the cube until you have filled the cube up to the top; see the illustration. Do one or two more cubes with the remaining soap mixture. You might want to make a few more batches of soap paste in different colors before putting the cubes aside to dry.

Find a warm, dry place to put the cubes for one or two days until the soap paste gets hard (test by pressing with your finger). Pop the SOAP CRAYONS out of the tray and they're ready to use. You will probably find that some colors work better than others, so try out the first batch yourself before passing the recipe on to a friend.

# Candy color circles

# Candy color circles

Many kids say this one is their favorite, and it's pretty obvious why. First you get to gather the recipe ingredients, and stir them up in a pot (kids love to stir). Then you watch the thick paste turn into a bubbly goo while deciding what colors to add. Finally comes the pouring of the big pancakelike lollypops, and the seemingly forever wait as they get hard. But in the end, you have big, bright and colorful CANDY COLOR CIRCLES. They can be hung in a sunny window so you can look out at a "rose-colored" world, or just let the color beams stream into the room. You might make a candy mobile, or decorate a tree, and when the time comes, you can eat them. Yum, yum.

INGREDIENTS          TOOLS

2 cups white sugar           cooking pot
1/2 cup light corn syrup     wood mixing spoon
1/4 cup water                aluminum foil
food coloring                candy thermometer
string                           (optional)

This recipe will make two 8-inch CANDY COLOR CIRCLES.

RECIPE

Making CANDY COLOR CIRCLES requires

cooking at high temperatures, so young kids must have help from someone who's older and allowed to use the stove. Cooking candy is best done when the weather is cool and dry. When it's very hot or humid, the candy can get sticky.

1) In a cooking pot, stir together the sugar, corn syrup, and water with a wooden spoon.

2) Put the pot over medium heat, and stir occasionally until the mixture begins to boil.

3) Attach the candy thermometer to the inside of the pot, making sure the thermometer bulb is in the mixture but not touching the sides or bottom of the pot. Let the mixture heat until the thermometer reads 310 degrees F. (hard crack). If you don't have a candy thermometer, use the water-drop method as follows: after the mixture has boiled for about five minutes, spoon out a small amount and let it drip into a cup of cold water. Keep testing this way until the ball that forms is hard and brittle—then the mixture is ready.

4) Remove the pot from the heat, and stir in the food coloring. About 20 to 40 drops should do, depending on how deep you want the color to be. You can use a single pure food color, or try mixing them to make

your own colors (blue plus red make purple).

5) Spread out a piece of aluminum foil, shiny side up. Before the mixture begins to harden, pour it out onto the aluminum foil in the shape of two big pancakes.

6) Now while the candy is still soft, poke 2 or 3 inches of a length of string into the top of each COLOR CIRCLE, as in the illustration. A toothpick or pencil is good for poking.

7) Let the circles cool for half an hour before removing them from the foil.

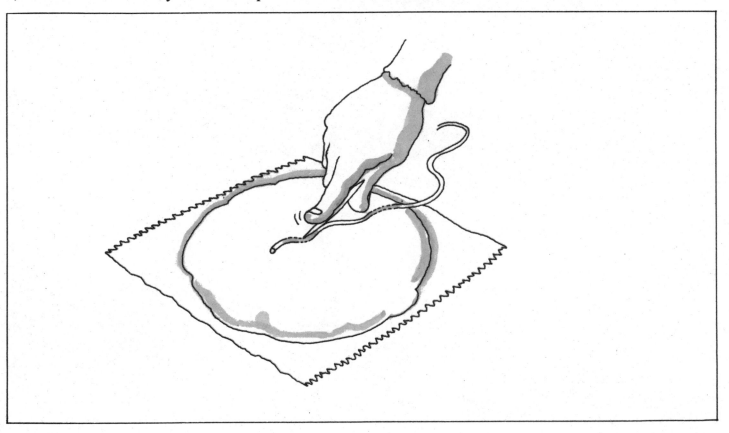

Design board

# Design board

There are no rules to tell you how to use a design board, and very little instruction is needed on how to make one. Anything goes. You can weave real or abstract designs, flat or "feeling" pictures. Designs of all sorts can be made with different kinds of string, yarn, thread, rubber bands, pipe cleaners, and so forth. Then you might weave in a feather, leaves or twigs—it's all up to you, the designer. A DESIGN BOARD can be made for keeps—a work of art to display—or it can come apart and be redesigned. A warning to parents is needed, however: it doesn't matter what the designs look like, or that they look like anything at all. Kids just enjoy expressing themselves in their own way.

MATERIALS          TOOLS

wood board          hammer
nails
string or yarn or rubber
    bands, or almost
    anything
scraps

## CONSTRUCTION

Hunt up a scrap wood board—something about 10 or 12 inches square and 1/2 or 3/4 inch thick is best if you have a choice, but nearly any size will do. Check to be sure there are no splinters or sharp edges. Randomly hammer a bunch of nails into one side of the board, keeping them at least 1 inch apart. The nails should be hammered in far enough so they hold, leaving about 1/2 inch of the nail sticking out; see the illustration. One-inch headed nails (called "common nails") do the job well. Now start designing.

Paperback sculpture

# Paperback sculpture

The Japanese have long been famous for the art of paper folding called origami. Here's a new twist. PAPERBACK SCULPTURE is the art of folding paperback book pages to make a sculpture *form* rather than a flat pattern. The fun and inventiveness is in experimenting with different ways to design and fold a book page. It's easy to do, and occupies a lot of time. In the end, you have a sculptured paper form that can be used as a decoration or the body of a people or animal doll.

Making PAPERBACK SCULPTURE can take a long time—repeating, as it does, the same folding pattern over and over again—so some kids may become a little impatient. If two or more kids can share in the work, however, then everyone may want a turn. PAPERBACK SCULPTURE is also a great project for someone sick in bed.

## MATERIALS

paperback book
paper clips

## CONSTRUCTION

Find an old paperback book, one you'll never need to read again. Pocket size paperbacks of about two hundred to four hundred numbered pages work best. You can waste a page or two experimenting with design patterns, but for your first PAPERBACK SCULPTURE do something simple, using no more than two or three folds per page. Once you've designed a pattern, fold every page exactly the same way. Instead of folding each page separately, you can do two or three pages at a time, but be consistent. If the covers are too stiff to fold, remove them or cut the covers

to the pattern shape with a scissors. Fan the book pages open in a circle, and paper clip, glue, or staple the covers together.

Once you've mastered the technique, try more complicated folds. Some kids like to make a card-board pattern and trace the folding lines on each page. That's not necessary unless you want the finished form to look perfect. Try using books with colorful pages, or fat magazines, and see what you can make.

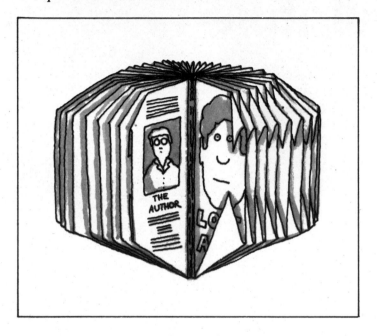

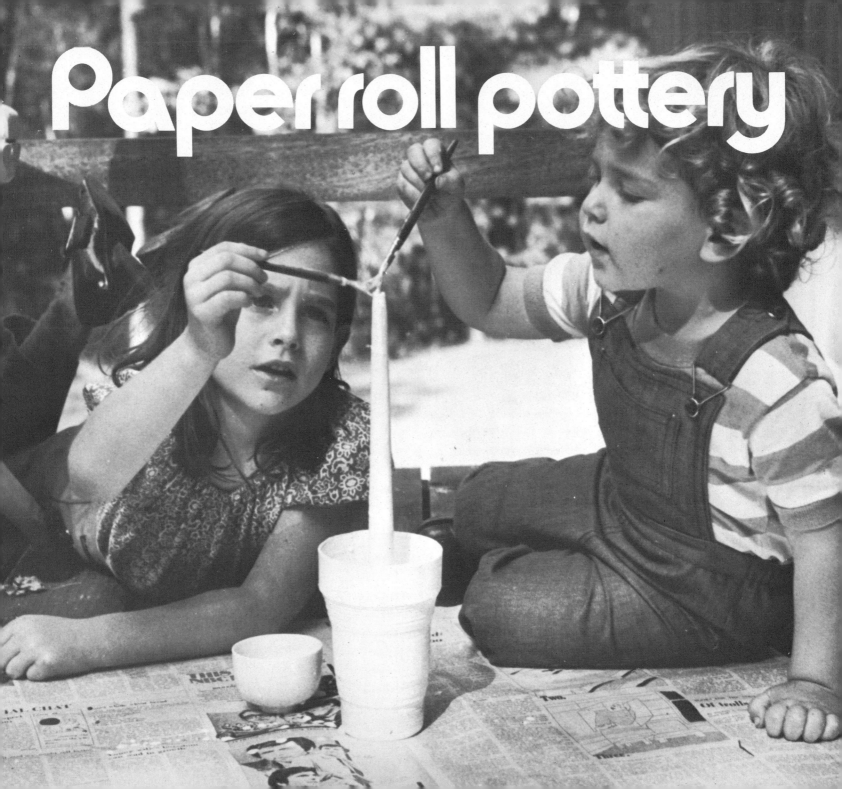

# Paper roll pottery

# Paper roll pottery

All kids enjoy doing clay pottery; they especially like oozing the clay through their fingers, and bending and shaping it into form. There's no substitute for that kind of play, but clay does have some drawbacks. Clay takes a long time to harden, and the clean-up can take longer than the potting. There is another neater and faster form of pottery making that uses only paper and glue, with finished products that can look very much the same as those of clay.

Among the things you can make are finger puppets, flowerpots, play tea sets, piggy banks, bowls, and sculptures. The forms can also be decorated with paint or color markers.

| MATERIALS | TOOLS |
| --- | --- |
| paper rolls (see below) | scissors |
| white glue | |
| tape | |

## CONSTRUCTION

The starting point of PAPER ROLL POTTERY is a spiral roll of paper. The size of the roll will determine the type of shapes you can make. A thick but small-around paper roll can make long, thin forms like a candlestick, and a thick, big-around paper roll can make a bowl shape.

Rolls of paper can be found, or you can easily make them. Some already-made paper rolls are: adding machine and cash register paper tapes, shelf paper rolls, and computer punch-tape rolls. Sometimes the paper rolls are wound too tightly, so you'll have to rewind them into looser rolls. The best thicknesses are between 1/2 inch and 1 inch. Sometimes the paper roll is too thick, so you'll have to cut it down. If you have to cut the roll down, unwind it while cutting the paper to

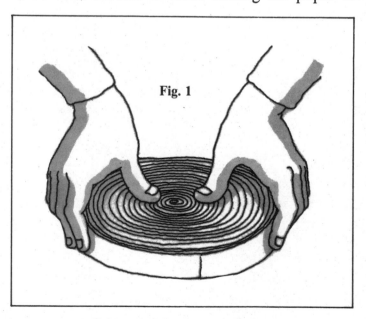

Fig. 1

# Reflection card

the proper size, then rewind the strip into a spiral roll.

It may be just as easy to make your own paper rolls. Cut even strips of paper from a newspaper, paper pad, magazine, or any smooth paper. Slightly overlap the strips and tape or glue them together. Wind the paper strips to make a spiral roll, and tape the end so the roll won't unravel.

Make the paper roll pottery by pressing the center of the roll out with your thumbs and fingers, Fig. 1, and easing the sides up and out.

Don't extend the roll too far, or the whole thing can fall apart. If you don't like a particular shape, you can flatten the coil again by pressing it down on a flat surface.

Start by forming something easy. When you're done, mix up a small cup of white glue with a little water, added for thinning. Spread the glue evenly and smoothly with your fingers over the entire surface of the pottery, inside and out. When the glue has dried, you can decorate as you wish.

Fig. 2

173

# REFLECTION CARD

It's interesting to see how reflectors of different shapes and sizes create a variety of patterns. Start with a smooth piece of aluminum foil, and cut it into reflector shapes like those in the illustrations, or like those you have invented in your mind. They can be dots, stripes, squares, or random shapes, big or little. Try not to crinkle the foil.

With just a tiny bit of glue (white glue, paper paste, mucilage, or glue stick) stick the foil parts, shiny side up, onto a piece of cardboard. The cardboard can be any size or shape.(The backs of large writing pads do well.) The darker the cardboard, the brighter the reflections will appear.

# Reflection card

Reflections often make beautiful picture patterns—the reflections of trees on a lake, or city buildings on a ripply street puddle. REFLECTION CARDS make beautiful light patterns that dance, stretch, bend, get big or small. You can make it all happen—you control the patterns and movement.

Hold a REFLECTION CARD under a bright light—the sun outside, sunlight streaming through a window, or a bright lamp. (You don't need to get very close to a light bulb.) Turn the card at different angles until the light bounces on a surface—the wall, ceiling, floor, tree, car, or yourself. Then bend, twist, and tilt the card to change the pattern. The closer you hold the card to a surface, the more distinct the pattern will be. The further you move from the surface the card is shining on, the fuzzier the pattern will get.

You can make many different REFLECTION CARD designs to produce different light patterns. Any design will work, but some are much more interesting than others. You'll have to experiment. Try using two cards of different designs, and have the reflected patterns mix together. Two or more kids can use cards at the same time, and create reflected light collages. They can even have light battles.

## MATERIALS

aluminum foil
cardboard
glue

## TOOLS

scissors

## CONSTRUCTION

Make more than one REFLECTION CARD.

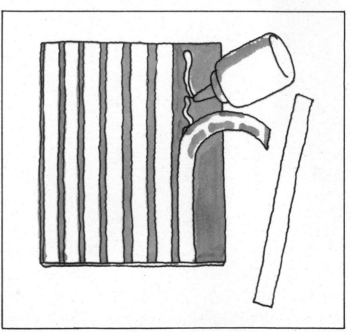